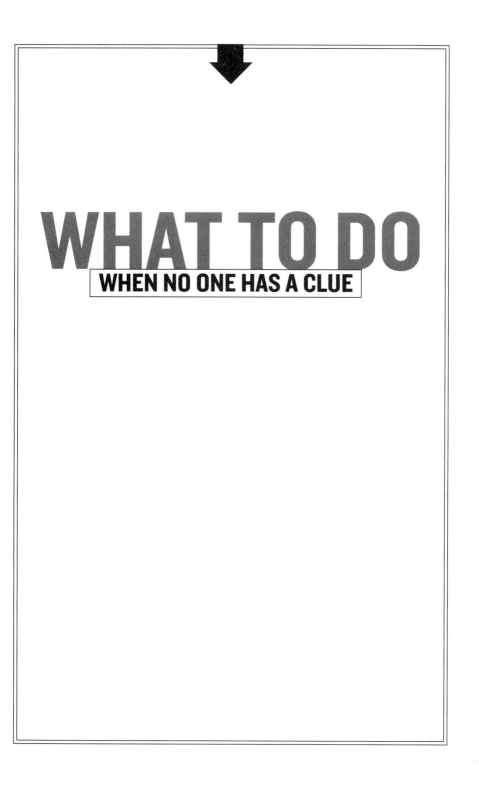

WHAT TO DO
WHEN NO ONE HAS A CLUE

WHAT TO DO
WHEN NO ONE HAS A CLUE

advice for the
brave new world ➡

STEPHANIE PIERSON AND **BARBARA HARRISON**

Clarkson Potter/Publishers

New York

Library of Congress Cataloging-in-Publication Data
Pierson, Stephanie.
    What to do when no one has a clue : advice for the brave new world
/ Stephanie Pierson and Barbara Harrison. — 1st ed.
        p.   cm.
    1. Conduct of life—Humor.   2. Technology—Humor.   3. Women—Humor.
I. Harrison, Barbara H.   II. Title.
PN6231.C36P54   2010
818'602—dc22   2009036989

ISBN 978-0-307-46320-3

Printed in the United States of America

DESIGN BY JANE TREUHAFT

10   9   8   7   6   5   4   3   2   1

First Edition

SP

For Lucy and Hazel,
who will know what to do.

BH

For Dan, Emily, Deborah, and Ben,
who know what to do.

CONTENTS

INTRODUCTION

We live in an energized, ever-changing, anything-goes, make-it-up-as-you-go world. It's life in the fast lane with no rules for the road.

From baffling questions: "What is she?" asks a stranger on the street when he sees you with your adopted Guatemalan daughter. "Mom, what do you think of my sex tape?" asks the teenage daughter who is proud of her national cinematic debut.

To bewildering choices: In a divorce, it used to be, Who gets the child? Now it's, Who gets the dog . . . your stepfather's ashes . . . the kabbalah coach?

From postdivorce, where your latest match from eHarmony turns out to be your ex.

To pre-op, where the hospital wants to know if you'd like to speak to the "orthopedic concierge" before your back surgery. (Will he or she be able to get you a room facing the park? A hospital robe from Frette? Hot theater tickets?)

Emotions are now emoticons (☺). The best technology (apps, blog crushes, Twitter recipes) makes us more human. Keyboard + Rant = Blog. Arianna Huffington + bloggers who don't get paid and love to do it = huge success.

Thanks to everything from tell-all blogs to tell-all books to live streaming video, the private is public. "Restraint" doesn't mean discretion, it means a court order against your ex. "Civil" doesn't mean your attitude, it means "court." The news doesn't break, it tweets. And it isn't really real until it's virtual.

At best, everything is totally confusing, and at worst, it's utterly perplexing. Even if you haven't faced one or another of these contemporary challenges, it's only a matter of time before you do. And you'll want to be ready with a response a little more helpful than "Uh . . . uh . . . huh?"

In this book, unprecedented situations find solutions from experts who examine and analyze the new, baffling, and bizarre on a daily basis. They—along with people whose unexpected experiences have turned them into social savants—share their advice on relationships, life choices, technology-induced challenges, family dynamics, living arrangements, social customs, business practices, birthing options, birthday options, pets, pet peeves, office dilemmas, burning culinary questions, medical practices, medical malpractices, life events, fashion queries, and gay marriage.

A renowned chef at a four-star restaurant tells you whether it's okay to ask for a doggie bag. The owner of two celeb hair salons shares what he thinks of "beauty makeover" parties for seven-year-old girls who have nothing to make over. An online medical expert tells you how to diagnose a possible case of terminal cyberchondria. A top dermatologist answers the question on everyone's lips: Is the injection that's made of pig collagen kosher?

From time to time, the experts beg to differ, but for the most part, there is one helpful answer on any given subject— along with the occasional aside that will illuminate things a bit further or just make you laugh.

While you are constantly being reassured in life that "you are not alone," frankly, you have been alone. Help is now here. Wisdom and wit are yours for the taking.

Read this book—take it with you everywhere—and you will never be the clueless one in the real world, the virtual world, the surreal world we live in.

HOW TO

TAME
TECHNOLOGY
[IMHO]

Today's technology has led to some profound and brilliant changes. Bunnies have blogs. People have avatars. The premier of China is on Facebook. So is Mother Teresa. You've always been able to divorce your parents, but now you can defriend them, too.

We crunch numbers. We know numbers. We store numbers. And so we have a number of new issues. "Now," says Jeremy Bailenson, director of Stanford's Virtual Human Interaction Lab, "the edge of the abyss is much closer in an era when so many people carry personal digital assistants containing hundreds of contact numbers—including those for clients, work adversaries, and bosses—everywhere, even to bars and parties." The result? Five rounds of tequila shots and one e-mail to your boss telling him why he's an asshole. The answer (aside from four fewer shots) is Google's Mail Goggles. Enable this app and you'll have to solve five simple math problems in sixty seconds in order to send any e-mail between ten P.M. and four A.M. on weekends.

We can make technology work for us: Twenty-year-old Dartmouth student Vanessa Sievers ran for treasurer of Grafton County, New Hampshire, and unseated the sixty-eight-year-old incumbent, Carol Elliott. Ms. Sievers's investment in her campaign was limited to the $51 Facebook advertisement she paid for herself. "I took advantage of new media and she did not," said Ms. Sievers.

We can use technology to widen our circles: When you're bored with the online friends who actually know you, Omegle .com will connect you with a random stranger for some anonymous, no-strings chat.

We have great technogadgets to guide us—Simultravel GPS, Google Earth, radio-frequency ID chips, iPhone map apps (and we have Google to thank for the term "searchology")—yet we still get lost.

We can even tame technology: Teresa Nielsen Hayden, a moderator at BoingBoing.net, is credited with a creative response to negative commentators: "disemvowelment," the removal of all vowels from a post.

The Internet is where we live. Proof of this is that homeless people who used to nod off for hours in Starbucks' cozy wing chairs are now in the Apple store using the MacBooks and listening to Coldplay.

Find out from the futurist, the founder of an online community, the time-management expert, the Apple trainer, the software engineer, the queen of online publishing, and the texting medical student when/where/how/to whom we can/should text it/tell it/tag it/tweet it/send it/delete it/call IT in a panic. ⇨

Who's got the right-of-way on a crowded sidewalk, the person using the CrackBerry or the person walking straight ahead who can see what's coming and step aside?

"It depends on whether the person walking straight ahead has an iPhone (they always get the right of way, at least according to Steve Jobs)." —ARIANNA HUFFINGTON, cofounder and editor in chief of the *Huffington Post*

Your intended wants to create a wedding blog that shares every detail with the whole world, from a photo of the bedroom you two share to a reminder for guests to appoint a designated driver so they can really enjoy the Moët & Chandon. You're more private. Do you have to say, "I do, too"?

"Clearly your intended didn't get the TMI memo. (I mean, really, your bed? That's a mental image your friends and family can live without.) The tricky thing here is that it's actually a positive thing that your fiancé is so enthusiastic about the wedding details, so you don't want to discourage him entirely. Instead, make the blog something you do together. He'll get to scratch his writing itch, and you'll have some editing power. If he still insists on blogging solo, he has every right to say what he wants—about himself. You, however, are completely within your rights requesting not to have details about you dished online. If he wants to go on and on about his tux, his groomsmen, or the band he found to rock your reception, that's fine. But your dress, your parents' wedding budget, and, yes, your bed are off-limits." —CARLEY RONEY, modern wedding and lifestyle expert; cofounder of America's leading wedding site, TheKnot.com; and author of *The Knot Book of Wedding Lists*

The coworker in the next stall is having an intense cell phone conversation. Can she talk? Can you flush?

"Talking on the phone while in the loo is the ultimate bathroom faux pas. First of all, who talks on the phone in the bathroom? There are a lot of very unpleasant noises coming out of that place, and the person on the other end of the line probably doesn't want to hear someone else during a delicate moment. It's definitely rude, and the only solution is for you to flush during the other person's conversation, preferably as many times as possible." —publishing copywriter AURORA SLOTHUS, who has overheard appallingly private conversations in her company's nineteenth-floor ladies' room

Is it okay to text bad news?

"A little bad, sure. Text messages are quick, and you can bet the person will read it almost instantly, while they may put off listening to a phone message until later. Breaking up with someone via text seems tacky. If it's really bad news—like, someone died—it's weird and inappropriate." —PHOEBE DAY, a twenty-seven-year-old medical school student who texts constantly and has taken courses about compassion in patient care

TECH AND TACKY: HOW TO AND WHY TO?

You can learn so much online. But maybe you shouldn't. DIY gets new meaning with the following projects on Instructables.com. The site's "How To" list includes "How to make a bicycle window box for the transient gardener," "How to build a Taser for free," and "How to make a sigh collector," which, in case you are not sure whether you need one, comes with a clear—well, maybe not completely clear—explanation of what it is: a home-monitoring system that measures and "collects" sighs. The result is a physical visualization of the amount of sighing, for personal use in a domestic environment. Oh. *Sigh.*

Are you antediluvian if you still have a landline? And are you worthy of walking the earth if you don't have a cell phone?
"'Landline'—does that have something to do with sailing?"
—A TWENTY-THREE-YEAR-OLD WRITER/bartender/SAT tutor
"Landlines confuse people because they don't understand why you didn't answer and/or get their text message while you were grocery shopping." —A TWENTY-SIX-YEAR-OLD BOSTONIAN who was forced to get a landline because her basement apartment doesn't get cell reception

Are you a criminal or a hero if you zap someone's cell phone call with a Spycatcher JAMIOI, a handy (and usually illegal) device that wipes out cell phone chatter within a fifty-foot radius?
"Legally, it depends on the state. If it isn't specifically prohibited, then you probably can use it. But there might be some federal law against it; you need to check. That being said,

there is also a moral issue. As long as cell phones are legal, what right do you have to cut off a conversation? And God forbid someone is calling with an emergency."
—STEVE LEIFMAN, associate administrative judge in Miami-Dade County, Florida
"Maybe instead you should just invest in some high-quality headphones. Or try actually asking the chatty perp to keep it down. Sure beats jail." —BEN FINKEL, founder and CEO of the online-community site Fluther.com

You're working toward an MBA because it's your best route to the career you want, the salary you expect, and the professional recognition you crave. Do you need to say that you are doing it online?
"No. For most programs, the degree is absolutely identical. The key is to get an online master's from a renowned bricks-and-ivy school that offers a distance-learning option. I won't tell if you don't!" —STEVEN HIRSCH, who advanced his career at IBM in exactly this way

You work in a computer store that also gives training sessions. While you're teaching a client something about download-ing documents, he inadvertently opens a file that reveals his colorful porn collection. Your response?
"Focus on what you're talking about—the specific computer question. Look straight ahead. Let them notice and close the window. It is awkward, but it happens all the time."
—an unflappable twenty-three-year-old COMPUTER TRAINER

You get an e-mail inviting you to reconnect with people from your past via Reunion.com. Do you really want to hear from that jerk who broke up with you the night before the prom or the person you fired ten years ago?

"No." —MICHAEL WINERIP, a Pulitzer Prize–winning reporter for the *New York Times*

Is it okay to text in church? During a business lunch? In Pilates class?

"If there's a human being nearby who deserves your attention, put away the handheld device. Same goes for driving or operating heavy equipment (presumably that doesn't apply to Pilates class). Otherwise, text away." —MARK HURST, founder of Creative Good and author of *Bit Literacy: Productivity in the Age of Information and E-mail Overload*

You've TiVo'd so many programs that you feel overwhelmed when you sit down to watch TV. What do you do about those hundreds of hours of *Oprah*, *Without a Trace*, and *The Daily Show*, not to mention twelve "can't miss" episodes of *30 Rock*, when all you really want to do is curl up with whatever *Law & Order* rerun is on right now?

"You need to think through your criteria for what you TiVo. Just because you can, doesn't mean you should. If you're recording to give yourself options, it can quickly become a burden instead. Ask yourself before you TiVo: Is it a show I follow closely and never miss an episode of? Is it just one particular episode I really want to see? Is it a "must" or is it just a "maybe"? And the most important question: When am I going to watch it? If you haven't watched it by Sunday night, clear out the TiVo box and start fresh." —JULIE MORGENSTERN, an internationally renowned organizing and time-management expert and the bestselling author of *Organizing from the Inside Out*

"Turn the clicker upside down behind your back, press three buttons, hit Enter, and watch whatever comes up. If you don't like your 'choice,' turn off the tube and go for a walk." —SCOTT FOLLIN, who gets 450 channels and whose TV is always on

You sure had a great time Saturday night, although the specifics are a hazy blur on Sunday when you crawl out of bed. Is your first move (after brewing strong coffee) to detag every incriminating photo that's already reached Facebook?

"Yes—but *before* brewing any coffee. I have a friend whose parents are fundamentalist Christians and would disown him if they found out he was drinking at college. After a long night of partying, he always sets his alarm for eight A.M. to make sure he is up to detag the pictures, hopefully before any of his relatives see them." —college student BILL NOVELLI

What do you do when the person next to you on an airplane doesn't shut off his or her phone and continues texting through the whole flight? Are we all going to crash because 14C wants to tweet?

From the seat: "Given the choice of saying something to the passenger or a flight attendant, which could conceivably lead to an altercation that might delay me one minute longer from the fun, interesting parts of the trip, I'd mind my own beeswax. Just turn the other cheek and feel less guilty for hogging the armrest." —ERIK TORKELLS, an editor for TripAdvisor.com and the editor of three travel books

Out of the gate: "The reason for this ban is the possible interference of a cell phone with the aircraft's communication and navigation systems, as well as the pilot's need to keep in touch with air traffic control. The point is that you're supposed to turn it off—not just for a phone call, but for texting and tweeting, too." —BETTY SKINNER, a ticket agent who has worked for American Airlines for thirty-five years

You are tempted to "jailbreak" your iPhone and install a fantastic new app that Apple hasn't approved. Are there any consequences? Does Steve Jobs really care? Is this just a modern version of the DO NOT REMOVE THIS TAG warning on your mattress? Or is it illegal?

"People started jailbreaking before Apple had the App Store. Explanations for how to do it and why to do it are all over

PLAYSTATION 3 SENTENCED TO PRISON

It turns out that PlayStation 3 isn't all fun and games. Some ingenious users have found a way to use it to the max, in maximum-security prisons! Authorities in England claim that technosavvy inmates are using the PlayStation to run massive crime syndicates. By using chat rooms in online games and communicating in coded language, prisoners are able to get information and orders to criminal coconspirators on the outside.

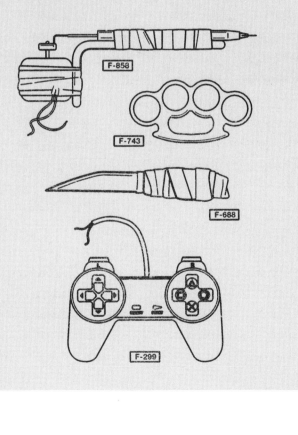

the Web. But yes, it really can result in Apple voiding your warranty." —A TRAINER at the Apple Store who needs to remain anonymous

"If Apple hasn't approved it, it's not that fantastic an app. Recovering a jailbreaked phone is a huge pain in the 'tocks. *Don't do eet!*" —the personal opinion of A WOMAN WHO WORKS FOR APPLE

You arrive at the hotel at eleven P.M., having guaranteed your room with a credit card for late arrival. The reservations manager informs you that they've given away your room because the online service you used didn't transfer the information, adding "It's not our fault."

"A Hyatt in Hawaii gave away our guaranteed room when our plane was late coming in. We made a big deal out of it, refusing to leave the desk and making a lot of noise. They ended up giving us the penthouse suite." —graphic designer and globe-trotter HEIDE FOLLIN, who makes all her travel arrangements online

"I shared the entire story—names, dates, and specifics—with the millions of consumers who rely on TripAdvisor. From that moment on, anyone looking for a hotel in Fort Washington, Pennsylvania, learned exactly why they should *not* stay at that hotel at any price. (P.S.: The hotel is now out of business.)" —business traveler RUSTY NOONAN, who admits that, sometimes, revenge is the best revenge

MY FI

One of the fun bonuses to piggybacking on someone's unsecured Wi-Fi is the chance to see what other people name their wireless networks. Among those observed by users of Fluther.com:

SexyTimeExplosion

Lenny the Leper

Virus (the message piggybackers get is "Connecting to Virus")

insertfreepornHERE

BlackDeath

Don't Steal

And the classic:

Get Your Own Fucking Internet

Are you cheap, smart, dishonest, or just recycling when you piggyback on a neighbor's wireless Internet service?

"That depends on how you use it. As long as you don't hog too much bandwidth, or do anything illicit, it's fine. It's up to your neighbors to protect their wireless connections, and they may be all right with sharing because there's no real cost to them. You could even offer to chip in to upgrade to a faster plan if you want to do it long term. But as long as you don't abuse your power, I say piggyback away." —BEN FINKEL, founder and CEO of the online-community site Fluther.com

"Just realize that whoever owns the network could be tracing your every e-banking move." —NEAL EPSTEIN, a software engineer who has a secured network

Is it okay to talk on your cell phone while you're having your hair done? After all, you're paying for it, and it's not like you're out with friends or a business colleague.
"If my cell phone rings, I usually answer it. If I don't attend to my clients at all times, I won't be able to afford the color and cut! But if the hairstylist is in the middle of a cut, I don't want to disturb his creativity, so I don't even look at who is calling. If it's important, I'm sure they will leave a message." —A TOP REAL ESTATE BROKER who sells houses to former presidents and CEOs of international banks

"No. It's rude. It pretty much says to the other person, 'I don't really acknowledge that you exist.' Unless you're waiting for a kidney transplant, you probably can turn off the phone for an hour without tragic results." —POOJA CHAUDRY, who is tethered to her BlackBerry for work but tries very hard to carve out some "real live person" time whenever possible

Is it snooping or savvy to scan public records for the truth/ secrets/dirt on a job applicant, babysitter, potential date, or that guy in the next cubicle whom you can't stand?
"If you're about to entrust someone with something as impor-tant as your business, your heart, or your kids, snoop away and get all the information you can. But if you just can't resist looking up how many speeding tickets your friends and enemies have gotten, do it but don't blab about it; if you do, people will know you're looking them up, too." —A HUMAN RESOURCES DIRECTOR for a major corporation

You are in a restaurant sitting three tables down from a Master of the Universe type who is on his cell phone, which is on "speaker." Ironically, he is sitting right under the universal sign that indicates no cell phone usage. The waiter says nothing, and the people sitting next to him say nothing—should you say something?

"I think you have a few options: One is to pull out a notebook very unsubtly, stare at him, and start taking notes whenever he says a name or place. Or, if he's not in your line of sight, ask the waiter to deliver a note saying that he's welcome to continue talking, but could he up the volume a little bit? You write for *Business-Week,* and you want to make sure you get the scoops he's discussing right. Or, if he's not talking about business and you're especially ballsy, just scoot your chair right up to his table, and when he inevitably asks what you're doing there, say that he was so loud that you weren't able to have your conversation at your table, so you thought you'd come over and join his." —AN EXECUTIVE HEADHUNTER who spends a great deal of her time in restaurants and is all too familiar with this kind of thoughtless, self-absorbed behavior

"*Should* you say something? Yes. *Would* you say something? Unless you're really bold and ballsy and willing to get into it with an obvious schmuck, probably not. Try asking the manager to say something. If he won't do it, then ask the maître d' to seat a large party with cranky children near this guy. Otherwise, suck it up. There are jerks everywhere, and this will make for an excellent cocktail party story."

—A FREELANCE WRITER who often takes her computer with her to coffee shops and neighborhood restaurants

Your dad sends the absolute worst joke e-mails, twice a week, to a huge list of people. They're not dirty jokes, just stupid and thoroughly not funny. You want to unsubscribe without hurting your father's feelings. But the worst part is that your friends, who are also on his list, want you to ask your dad to unsubscribe them, too. What do you do?

"Rather than ask him to take me off his list, I just delete the messages as they arrive in my in-box. As lame as it is, it's his way of keeping in touch." —A WOMAN who has been inundated with these e-mails for at least five years

"Tell him you're deluged with e-mails . . . truly wish you had time to read them but really haven't got a second. Thank him for understanding and taking you off his list. As to also removing your neighbor/friend/whomever, tell him you know they don't like to receive mass e-mails. If that doesn't work, I have found from personal experience—and after a couple of courteous but completely futile requests to be taken off e-mail lists—that a really angry e-mail reply will do the trick. (Capital letters help. One begins with STOP SENDING ME MASS E-MAILS and continues from there.) Hurt feelings? Aaaaagh! The deluged recipient stops caring after a certain point."

—HELEN CHAYEFSKY, who spends most of her working hours and much of her private time online, not sharing lame jokes

2

HOW TO

MAKE IT EVENTFUL

[FROM BOTOX PARTIES TO WEDDINGS]

Well, of course we know what to give for Valentine's Day. But what's the right present for a Bark Mitzvah? For the eight-year-old girl whose granola mom is giving her a "learn to knit a bookmark" birthday party? For a coming-out-of-prison party? For a pet psychic party where the psychic will "read" paws?

Life is, of course, a gift, but the rest is pretty confusing. What to buy for your mom's third wedding? Your best friend's second daughter's fifth engagement party? Your ex-sister-in-law's divorce party? Are home-baked cookies the ideal gift for the homeless shelter's holiday gathering?

Of all the choices that confuse and confound, weddings take the cake. Or the jelly mold. Would you, the early-adopter bride, be inclined to order from London's Bompas & Parr a trendy wedding jelly, a huge wobbly tower of Jell-O perfect for "brides keen to avoid stodgy wedding cakes"? The creators of this non–Martha Stewart confection add that these gelatin desserts are "kinder to the stomach after a heavy meal so make it less likely for guests to fall asleep during the speeches!" Will your wedding guests be speechless if the Ukrainian pastry chef/groom whips up, for his fiancée, a twenty-pound wedding dress made up of fifteen hundred cream puffs? Will flour, eggs, sugar, and caramel be the new *peau de soie* or French organza? (Neatorama.com) And, on a less extravagant scale, do you agree that nothing screams romance like an "unusual wedding bouquet mousepad"? (Zazzle.com)

The right host or hostess gift sounds simple. Of course, there's nothing wrong with the usual suspects: chocolates, flowers, wine, a small but pricey jar of jam (*yawn*). But what if the gift involves a trip abroad? A thoughtful traveler from Orlando recently returned from a trip to Germany and shared this suggestion: "We shipped a case of Charmin bath tissue to the friends we were to spend several days with. It was extremely well received." (Ricksteves.com) *Chic alors!* As the recipient, should you be offended if your mother-in-law thanks you for the weekend with a book about how to save your marriage? Will your dinner party hostess LOL if you give her an apron that reads, "I can go from Hostess to Bitch in 2.3 seconds"? (Prankplace.com) Or should you just get the board game that lets you and your friends choose the presents you would give each other if you were actually giving presents so you never have to give a present at all? (Gametrap.co.uk)

You're cordially invited to clear up any confusion and get the party started with advice from bridal specialists, event planners, ministers and rabbis, Botox party girls, a magazine editor, a chic boutique owner, a celebrity stylist, a fashion designer, a financial adviser, a live-wire funeral director, and a bride with a transgendered bridesmaid. ▷

In lieu of wedding gifts (they haven't registered anywhere), the happy couple asks that you make a charitable contribution to their favorite animal shelter. But you'd rather give them a silver bowl. What should you do?

"Do you have something against puppies? If the couple wants you to donate to the charity of their choice, embrace it. They may already own most of the typical registry items—especially if they live together. Also, think about why you want to purchase something in the first place. Are you more concerned with your friends having tangible evidence that you purchased something? Trust me, they'll be notified when you make a charitable donation." —CARLEY RONEY, modern wedding and lifestyle expert, cofounder of TheKnot.com, and author of *The Knot Book of Wedding Lists*

"My suggestion would be to abide by their request. But if you can't do that, give a token donation to the animal shelter. And send the silver bowl with a little note reading, 'We couldn't resist!'" —MARCY BLUM, celebrity wedding and event producer

The bride confides in you, her best friend, that she wants to live out her "red-carpet fantasies" on her wedding day in a bridal gown that leaves almost nothing to the imagination. Your advice?

"Is her red-carpet fantasy just a difference in personal taste or a potential disaster? If it's a disaster in the making, you should probably say something. But keep this in mind: She's probably already getting a lot of unsolicited advice. If you do say something, make sure she understands that you're bringing it up because you care about her. My own unsolicited advice? A lot of brides are wearing one dress for the ceremony and a different one for the reception. (And sometimes a third one for the after-party!) She may be able to live out her fantasy later at night, once the parents have left for the evening and she's surrounded by her close friends." —Bee Kim, founder of the popular wedding site Weddingbee.com

"If she's got fabulous fake boobs she wants to flaunt, let her. If she wants to show off a back that took a personal trainer six months to tone, she should go for it. This is not the era of *The Princess Bride*. And everyone from Vera Wang to Priscilla of Boston is designing dresses that show off a bride's figure." —a beautiful, buxom, and buff beauty who has gone to four weddings in six months

The soon-to-be-married couple has registered only at Tiffany and Registerstock.com and you've been out of work for six months. How do you go to the wedding without being known as "that cheap friend"?

"There's no law that says you have to give something from their registry. In this case, I'd suggest getting them something practical, like a toaster—something completely outside the parameters they've set up themselves. In that way, you don't compete in a contest you can't win. And, frankly, who can't use a good toaster?" —Franklin Getchell, co-owner and president of Moss, a mecca for sophisticated wedding shoppers in search of one-of-a-kind gifts

"What seems wildly extravagant to some may seem perfectly normal to someone else. So if you don't see anything on the registry that fits your budget or your idea of an appropriate gift, it's perfectly okay to go off-registry." —Amanda Clayman, a psychotherapist who specializes in financial wellness

SLUMBER PARTIES

Invitations come in all forms: formal, Facebook, Evite, e-mail, personalized magnets, and now somnambulant e-mails. The already classic case of "tech-no memory" and a most un-expected party invitation comes from a forty-four-year-old woman who went to bed early one night, got up a few hours later, walked into the next room, and sat down at her computer. She turned it on, connected to the Internet, and—still asleep—logged on with her user name and password, then composed three e-mails—one of which read, "Come tomorrow and sort this hellhole out. Dinner and drinks, 4 P.M. Bring wine and caviar only." The next day, she had no memory of her actions and found out what she had done only when one of the invitees called her to accept the invitation. (Scientists believe that somnambulistic episodes may be triggered by certain prescription medication.) Hopefully, the hapless hostess was awake for the party.

You get a "Save the Date" fridge magnet but the actual invitation to the wedding never arrives. Now what?

"Update your Rolodex and expect the engagement gift to be returned! Or—and more seriously—you can graciously give the bride or groom a call and see if *their* Rolodex is updated." —COLIN COWIE, author of seven bestselling books on lifestyle and events, including weddings

"Our babysitter's sister—whom we met only once—sent us a fancy engraved 'Save the Date' card. But no invitation ever arrived. I never said a word, and was very happy not to have to go or send a gift to someone I barely knew." —BETH HAYES, who that year had already bought nine Bar Mitzvah, six wedding, and four anniversary presents

How do you include your best friend, "Carl"—who six months ago was still "Carrie"—in your traditional wedding party of three bridesmaids and three groomsmen?

"We had exactly this situation. We decided to mix it up to keep the focus off 'is she/he or isn't she/he?' by standing two bridesmaids and one groomsman (not Carl) at the bride's side, and two groomsmen (including Carl) plus one bridesmaid at the groom's side. Gender issues disappeared and everyone was comfortable." –newlyweds HOWARD ARONSON and MELODY MARTIN

Two lesbians are planning their wedding. Each bride-to-be wants to have six bridesmaids. How many is too many? Should all twelve bridesmaids wear the same dress style? And are bridesmaid dresses cheaper by the dozen?

"The ultimate matchy-matchy nightmare would be all twelve bridesmaids in the exact same dress and the exact same color. I would suggest a combination of a few similar styles and then maybe six ladies in one color and the other six in a slightly different shade. Like a deep purple offset by lavender, or bright pink and a soft pink. And in most boutiques it *is* cheaper by the dozen! There are usually discounts offered to larger parties. Then, of course, there's the question of what each bride wears. We're seeing a trend where each bride wears a dress—one might be more sporty and kicky and the other more romantic. The dresses could be coordinated in some nuanced way—with a band of the same color or a piece of the same lace."

—A FORMER BRIDAL STYLIST at chic Amsale who created the stunning silk faille bridal gown featured in the movie *27 Dresses*

Your best friend is getting married for the second time in three years, and you still haven't found your first True Love. What are you expected to do about a gift? And do you have to throw her (another) bridal shower?

"Yes, she has found two Mr. Rights to your zero (or maybe she's just found two Mr. Right Nows), but this is still your best friend, and she deserves a gift for her celebration. Of course, if the whole situation makes you truly uncomfortable, you can simply say, 'You are my best friend and I love you. In lieu of another big fancy platter from Tiffany's, I am donating money in your name to [fill in the blank] charity'—choose one that has some sort of link or tie to her. As far as a shower, it's unlikely that someone getting married for the second time in three years will want another big shindig. If you feel obligated to throw her something, do a simple tea with only very close friends or a nice dinner out. Absolutely no ribbon hats should be made!" —JOURNALIST CAROLINE DEL COL, who writes and edits relationship articles for women's magazines and has attended dozens of bridal showers

The bride asks you and her other bridesmaids to get Botox, whiten your teeth, and go to a tanning salon before her Big Day. Can you refuse the "honor"? And how do you do it tactfully?

"I think one can gently decline, letting her know that the last thing you want is to upstage her with blinding teeth, an orange bod, and the inability to show emotion (multiplied by four bridesmaids or, in the case of this woman, probably twelve)." —LISA SILVERMAN MEYERS, a seven-time bridesmaid and one-time bride

A.

B.

What's out of bounds when you're throwing a bridal shower for a twenty-something knowing that her mother and eighty-five-year-old grandmother will be there, too?

"In cases where the hostess may have a more risqué theme for the shower (i.e., guests should bring gifts of lingerie or maybe sex toys), I would suggest opening them *after* Mom and Grandmom have departed. Ask your guests to mark their gifts if they contain risqué content—although if Gran and Mom are hip and young or young at heart, they might like the excitement. You need to decide what makes sense and go with that."
—Colin Cowie, an arbiter of style, widely known for throwing the most spectacular celebrations across the globe

"Don't even *think* of serving penis-shaped pasta. I was mortified when the penises-with-pesto came out of the kitchen. Even a surprise shower shouldn't have the sort of X-rated surprises that could embarrass anyone." —recently married Karen Krause

One of the bridesmaids-to-be has a prominent tattoo of a tree that goes up her back and explodes into branches with intricate and colorful foliage. How much attention will this body art divert from the bride? And what kind of dress could the bridesmaid wear to keep this from happening?

"Bridesmaids are individuals. This is why they are an important part of the special day. At the start of the ceremony, the tatted bridesmaid may get some extra glances, but the moment the bride begins her walk down the aisle, guests will be saying, 'Whose tattoo?' Body makeup is available in most cosmetics stores, some specifically for tattoo cover-ups. Or the bride could have all of her girls in a bolero or shawl during the ceremony." —AN ORANGE COUNTY BRIDAL STYLIST

"You want to respect the bride, and it's easier than ever to do that. Bridesmaids today are wearing dresses from the same collection, but they don't have to wear the exact same style. While the fabric and hemline of their dresses are alike, the color palette can be slightly varied—say, nuanced shades of yellow. So the tattooed bridesmaid can swan down the aisle in a gorgeous dress that has a bit more coverage in the back and not worry about upstaging the bride." —JIN WANG, a San Francisco fashion designer whose collection includes sophisticated bridal gowns and bridesmaids' dresses

Your friend's daughter is having one engagement party, two bridal showers, a "welcome to the groom's family" brunch, and a destination wedding in Venice. How many events are you expected to attend?

"Not everyone can afford to attend a destination wedding in Venice, let alone all those prewedding parties. Most couples throwing a destination wedding understand that not everyone can make it. Your friends may be more understanding than you think if you have to decline. Remember, you are not expected to bring a gift to every event, but if you choose to do so, a great idea is a gift that has several parts—like china or utensils. Portions of the gift can be given at each event, with a hint in the first gift indicating that more is to come."

—BEE KIM, founder of the popular wedding site Weddingbee.com

Should you let your seven-year-old daughter go to a salon party where all the girls get "makeovers" years before they have anything to make over? Or is it just fun and not something that will thwart the child's future as an independent woman who reads Balzac's novels in French?

"I have done lots of parties for seven-year-olds, but I wouldn't call them 'makeovers.' Little girls love playing dress-up. It's a whole 'Mommy and Me' fantasy experience. We have a great time doing it. Of course, we don't do anything extreme—it can be as simple as putting a little braid in their hair."

—LOUIS LICARI, owner of hair salons in New York and Beverly Hills and the star of NBC's *Ambush Makeover*

You learn that a friend is hosting a Passion Party (Passion Parties.com) so her girlfriends can buy the sexy toys and lingerie that promise to "make every day Valentine's Day." When you realize that you're not invited, are you flattered (She thinks I'm sexy enough!), insulted (I'm a prude?), or relieved (Whew! I'd never be able to look at Marla again after knowing what she does with white-chocolate-flavored body pudding)?

"I'd be a little hurt to be left out. But I would instantly convert that emotion into mild self-righteousness, passing judgment on her for hosting such a cheesy party. I like banana-flavored body paint as much as the next gal, but the idea of a Passion Party sounds like hell to me. I guess I *am* a prude."
—A TWENTY-NINE-YEAR-OLD who is almost always up for a party

You're invited to your own parent's second (or third) wedding. What would be a nice gift, without being too weird, since the Cuisinart, the Calphalon, and the heirloom crystal are already in the cupboard?
"The nicest gift would be something inclusive of the new spouse. A framed picture with all of you in it. Or tickets to a concert for all of you. Anything that shows you are happy for them and want to share in their happiness." —MARCY BLUM, whose bridal advice is often found in *InStyle Weddings, Modern Bride,* and the *New York Times*

MAKE IT A DIVORCE TO REMEMBER

While some might call it a "failed marriage," there's no reason you can't have a really successful divorce. Have fun: Throw a classy divorce party, complete with male strippers (Greysons .com). Be a little flexible about the facts: Go on Match.com and announce that you have never been married. Be proactive: Go for a "Grow a Lover" ($2 each). Just drop him in a glass of water and your new companion grows up to six hundred times his diminutive start-up size. (And probably doesn't come with mini meddling in-laws!)

Do you have to obey an invitation's directive to wear "creative black tie," "hacienda chic," "masquerade," or "boho luxe"? And what are those, anyway?

"You should honor your hosts' request regarding attire, but they should be clear about what they expect from you. We don't know what these styles mean either, so feel free to interpret them however you want." —red-carpet favorites Mark Badgley and James Mischka of Badgley Mischka, hailed by *Vogue* as one of the "Top 10 American designers" for their glamorous, elegant evening wear and accessories

You want to surprise your wedding guests by having the first dance be a sexy, sexy Al Green song. Your mother is thinking Stevie Wonder. And your grandmother is hoping for Cole Porter. Who gets to name that tune?

"It might sound like a cliché, but whatever is unique about the couple should be celebrated, Al Green included. On the other hand, you don't want to make a choice that will crush the grandmother who dipped into her life savings and spent $15,000 on your wedding dress." —James Abel, who has planned weddings in locations from the British Virgin Islands to Maui to Manhattan

Traditionally, your relatives have given the Bar Mitzvah boy blue-chip stocks. Is stock still a good gift these days, or does it just look like you're unloading?

"What we used to call blue-chip stocks are now the penny stocks, and you really don't want to give worthless pieces of paper, do you? If you do want to give stock as a teaching tool, then choose something the child would know, like Apple or Coca-Cola. But these days, savings bonds and cash are often the gift of choice." —financial adviser Carole Epstein, of Morgan Stanley Smith Barney

The last funeral you went to had ice cream at the grave site (the deceased had driven an ice cream truck). The most recent memorial service you attended was held on the eighteenth green (she went to the golf course on Sundays instead of to church). When it comes to death, should you put the "fun" in "funeral"?

"Today's services are much more about 'celebrating a life' than they are about 'mourning a death.' It is much more comforting to people when the service is something they can relate to and participate in. They won't remember the prayers or the service—but they'll definitely remember the ice cream truck!"
—Ron Hast, a funeral director for more than fifty years and the publisher of *Mortuary Management* magazine

You're throwing a birthday party for your eight-year-old son. The place you're having his laser tag party is charging you $15 per child. Three of the fathers who drop off their sons see the action and decide they want to stay and play, too. Are you expected to pay for these big children?

"You don't 'have' to do anything. If you can swing it, you should let everyone play, in a 'the more the merrier' spirit of generosity and party karma. If you can't, or don't want to for whatever reason, you should tell the fathers (or deputize a friend to tell them) that you're not allowed any more people on your plan with the management, but that they should go ask whoever's working and see what it would take for them to get in on the action. Wish them luck with their negotiations."
—Ada Calhoun, editor in chief of Babble.com and author of *Instinctive Parenting*

"Invitations are great for spelling out very clearly the things you would rather not have to say in person. If you need to, let the parents know in bold caps that the party is in fact a drop-off affair." —Pilar Guzmán, former editor in chief of *Cookie* magazine

DWI (DRIVING WHILE INTOXICATED) AND OWS (ONLINE WHILE STUPID)

Shortly after his arrest on a drunk-driving charge, twenty-year-old Joshua Lipton decided to go to a Halloween party dressed as a prisoner. Someone at the party took pictures of him—in a black-and-white striped shirt and an orange jumpsuit—and posted them on Facebook, labeled "Jailbird." The prosecuting attorney on Lipton's drunk-driving case used the pictures in court as evidence of the defendant's lack of remorse while his seriously injured victim was still in the hospital. The judge sentenced the "prisoner" to prison for two years.

Now that you don't need a life event to register for the gifts you really want, should you let potential gift givers know what you want for your birthday, for Halloween, for Christmas, or just because they love you? And how do you announce this good news to the world?

"When my college roommate went to Togo with the Peace Corps, she made an Amazon.com wish list of books she hadn't seen or read. This way, anyone who cared enough to mail her a present didn't have to risk shipping yet another copy of *Everything Is Illuminated* to Africa. I kind of appreciated that she made it so easy." —A RECENTLY ENGAGED WOMAN who is happy to share all joys, large and small

The bride grew up hyphenated and so did the groom. Now they're getting married. What to do about their names?

"The lovely thing about names is that you really have creative license to change them to whatever you want and name yourselves and your kids whatever you choose. If the bride wants to keep her name, there will be no debate. If she wants to take her husband's name, she can take his hyphenated name and drop hers. Or he can take hers and drop his own! Or if they are really creative—and I know couples who have done this—they can combine them all into one blended name that they both take together." —A JOURNALIST in her early thirties whose friends have found a variety of satisfying solutions

"Marriage is a union, and, as such, names become part of that union. Either stick to one name or carve out a new one. Keep in mind that each state has different laws regarding hyphenation and name changing, so check with your county clerk before making this an issue!" —interfaith minister SHARAN DePALMA of Chappaqua, New York

"The real shared experience comes when both bride and groom explain to one parent why they're dropping his or her last name but not the other." —newlywed DEBORAH POOLE

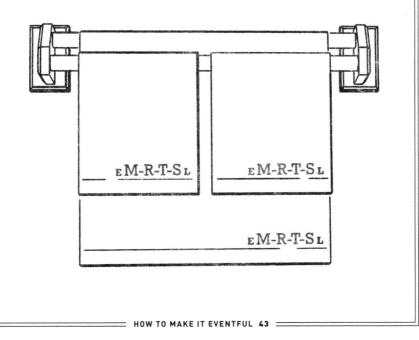

At your cousin's wedding, the rabbi called the bride by the wrong name. At your college roommate's wedding, the minister spoke at length about how many couples end up divorced. Now you're engaged and wonder, what's my best defense against a ceremony that makes the bridal couple, and the guests, cringe?

"This is not the occasion when you want to be surprised. So interview the officiant thoroughly before hiring him or her. Be open and honest about what you want on your wedding day. I write out each ceremony and e-mail it to the couple a week before the wedding, so they can make changes. Once you're in the middle of a ceremony and the officiant goes off script, however, there's not much you can do beyond sending a piercing stern look. By the way, sometimes the officiant is the one who is surprised: I went to a formal rehearsal dinner where the groom's sweet—but slightly tipsy—ex-girlfriend made a lovely toast to the happy couple, then proceeded to launch into a diatribe about why she was so much prettier and sexier than the bride-to-be and concluded by saying that she should be the one getting married instead." —A LICENSED INTERFAITH WEDDING OFFICIANT who knows that life, even with careful advance planning, is full of surprises

MARRYYOURPET.COM

Enough said.

3

HOW TO

DATE

[MATCHING, MEETING,
AND MATING]

When the Internet first reared its high-tech head, a *New Yorker* cartoon said it all: "In cyberspace, no one knows you're a dog." Relationships today, online and off, tend to be murky, muddled, and confusing, even for (especially for) the two (or more!) involved.

How do you even tell if you *are* involved? Someone asks if the two of you are dating, and in spite of the fact that you know each other, have been out together, and have slept with each other, you aren't sure. Are you hanging out? Are you just hooking up? Is it a relationship? And why is it that "hooking up" always goes with "just"?

On the other hand, some relationships are *too* clear. Leaving no doubt in anyone's mind, a *New York Times* wedding announcement coyly reveals that the bride and groom had never been attracted to each other "in that way." Then they traveled to Spain as friends . . . shared a room because there was only one left at the Parador . . . and by the next morning, they were a couple—attributing it at least in part to "that bottle of Rioja."

Fortunately, you don't have to endure your mother's efforts to fix you up with her yoga teacher's brother/cousin's math tutor/hairstylist's dentist because there are total strangers willing to do it, for a fee. From Patti Stanger (the star of Bravo TV's *The Millionaire Matchmaker*) to Samantha Daniels, attorney-turned-matchmaker (MatchmakerintheKnow.blogspot.com), the experts can find that high-quality, wealthy soul mate who's eluded you so far but who will love you for who you are. As long as you change your hair color/lose weight/get contacts/

fix your teeth/replace your wardrobe/rethink your behavior/ revamp your life goals/relocate.

But however you meet your mate, true romance can be false. French-born Thierry Khalfa, who now lives in Florida, said the reason he copied from screenwriter Mike Matteo's online profile was because his own English isn't so good. When he was caught and promptly dumped by a woman who, through sheer coincidence, turned out to be a friend of Mr. Matteo's, Mr. Khalfa said, "That guy should be proud. In France, in the fashion business, when you see something that looks good, you take it and copy it." When pressed, he added, "After all, I'm not Cyrano de Bergerac."

When arranged marriages start looking really good, you could use some really good advice from a dating coach, a love-life-management specialist, a relationship and sexuality expert, a matchmaker, a dating guru, the creator of an online dating system, a human behavior researcher, and an online dater. ▷

You've just discovered that one of your parents is dating one of your friends. Is there anything you can/should/shouldn't say to one or the other of them? Is there any way not to feel like you are in some weird Judd Apatow movie?

"It's really hard. The most common reaction is to be totally turned off by just the thought of our parents' sexuality, much less the idea of them poaching into our age group. Once that veil is lifted, we can't have the distance we need to process it. A normal reaction is to feel disturbed and angry."

—Pepper Schwartz, PhD, a University of Washington sociologist, the author of fourteen books about relationships, and a sexuality adviser for WebMD

"Politely suggest that your parent and friend refrain from PDAs in front of you. (PDAs in this case include hugging, kissing, touching, and making eye contact.) Also, make a lot of fake barfing noises to your other friends when discussing

this relationship. You can be pretty sure that the life span of this relationship is not going to require an eternity ring."
—twenty-seven-year-old JEAN DUNHILL, whose father's girlfriends get younger and younger the older he gets

When is it okay to lie when you are dating online? If everyone else is adding inches, subtracting years, and "borrowing" a better-looking photo, does the unvarnished truth guarantee that you'll spend Saturday night with the TV and takeout?
"If you're in your twenties: You don't need to lie about (A) your age, (B) how much you exercise, or (C) what you earn. If you're in your thirties: You can lie about C, but not about A or B. If you're in your forties or older: You can lie about any of the above. If you've been married before: Don't lie. It'll come out later, and it will definitely be awkward. If you're a big drinker, you should probably lie about it, unless you're a twenty-five-year-old female looking for a raging football fan."
—LYNN EMORY, who dated half of Atlanta's eligible bachelors online before she met her fiancé on Match.com

Should you admit to your friends that you often check out BeautifulPeople.net and HotorNot.com?
"Oh, sure, as long as you couch it as a sociological study of the low standards of modern society. And just act like it's no big deal. For example: 'I was looking at BeautifulPeople.net the other day, just because I couldn't believe that a site like that even exists! What is the world coming to?'(Note: You can only use that once. After the third try, you'll just have to fess up that you love it.)" —ANIKA CHAPIN, an assistant theater director

SORRY I ASKED

Your fifteen-year-old daughter has started dating a boy who's old enough to have a driver's license. She tells you the kind of thing every parent hopes to hear: "Guess what? Mike doesn't drink!" When she sees how pleased the news makes you, she excitedly adds, "He's in AA!"

It's the first date. Does she have to admit that her boobs aren't real? Does he have to admit that he's taking Viagra?

"It's none of their @#$% business! Some of the best plastic surgery jobs look really amazing these days, and he should be glad he's even getting boobs! Same goes for the man. Why admit anything? Sooner or later, every guy's going to need some help." —PATTI STANGER, star of the Bravo TV series *The Millionaire Matchmaker*

"My advice: Get the guy first. After you snag him, you'll have plenty of time to confess." —BAMBE LEVINE, founder of Bambe Levine Public Relations, who advises clients about when to speak up and when to shut up

You've found a real catch who is smart and sexy, and has a huge walk-in closet. Should you move in with someone you've been dating for only a few months because your lease is up?

"Only if that person is a really good cook. Seriously, moving in together needs to be more than a business decision. It's not about whether your rent is going down or going up. Real estate markets—like romance—are extremely changeable. So follow your heart." —MILES CHAPIN, associate broker at Warburg Realty

"Travel light and be agile." —A COSMOPOLITAN TWENTY-SEVEN-YEAR-OLD WOMAN who understands the vagaries of love and the pragmatism of real estate

You're not so good at tooting your own horn. And besides, you don't have all that much to toot about yet. Is it okay to "borrow" from someone's personal profile for your online dating and social networking space?
"Lots of people do it, but that doesn't make it right. It's theft, it's plagiarism, and it dilutes the value of the person who wrote it. You are stealing someone else's heart and soul. What if I took your résumé and presented it as my own because we have similar careers? Or used your photo as my own because we sort of look alike?" —EVAN MARC KATZ, dating coach, author of *Why You're Still Single,* and creator of the online dating system FindingTheOneOnline.com

Your partner insists that if it's really love, you'll share your computer password as "a sign of trust." Should you?
"No. You should say, 'If you love me, you'll respect my privacy.' And if he keeps pushing with something as fundamental as this, dump the loser." —DANIEL JONES, editor of the "Modern Love" column in the *New York Times*

If you Google your date before you go out—and who doesn't?—should you admit it or pretend you know nothing about the other person?
"Some Googling ground rules:

1. If you discover anything truly embarrassing, or worse, don't mention it. This includes 'before' photos that reveal some kind of dramatic physical transformation, et cetera.
2. If you discover something really funny that is unrelated, such as a child star who shares the same name or something, then go ahead. A guy once revealed to me that there is a racehorse who shares my full name. As a person who is no stranger to self-Googling, I was totally delighted, as it was news to me.
3. Never reveal the extent to which you researched the person, or the extent to which the results interested you. I always pretend the details are a little hazy in my mind."

—HAPPY MENOCAL, an illustrator who checks out everything from her date's fantasy baseball stats to his mother's maiden name ahead of time

Is phone sex "cheating"?
"Yes. The people on both ends of the phone line are very real. But it's not as bad as actual (live) cheating."
—love-life-management specialist NANCY SLOTNICK, a former consultant for JDate whose website, Cablight.com, claims to help a woman find the man of her dreams in less than six months

How soon after you meet someone can you add the person as a friend on Facebook without being branded a loser or a stalker?
"Move it or lose it. Friending someone right after you've met them helps you keep track of the person, should you run into him or her again. If you wait a few days and then friend them,

that's equivalent to saying, 'I've been thinking about you for days.' This is probably not the message you want to send."
—A TWENTY-THREE-YEAR-OLD PARALEGAL who actively networks and updates his status at least once every day

Do you tell the person you've just started dating that you previously swung the other way?
"I wouldn't. It's like dropping a bomb. The peacock shimmers his feathers to attract; he doesn't drop bombs. So I'd act like a good primate and show the glowing side of my moon. I don't tell a man anything at all about my previous dating experiences. And until I ask, I hope he doesn't tell me either— unless it is something I need to know before I consider going out with him." —HELEN FISHER, PhD, the relationship expert called "the dating guru" by *People* magazine and chief scientific adviser to Chemistry.com

"This is one of those 'need-to-know basis' situations. Unless there's a good reason, most people—while initially turned on—will be threatened. And don't do it unless you are prepared to hear that your date has a similar history."
—A GAY THERAPIST whose practice is 90 percent gay

WEDDING BELLES

A fifty-something woman heard that her favorite niece had just gotten engaged. She promptly placed a congratulatory call to her niece and asked excitedly, "Who's the lucky man?" "Maureen," the bride-to-be replied.

Your best friend has been in a committed relationship for a year. Then you spot her significant other's profile on Match.com. Do you tell your friend? Or her partner?

"Yes, you should tell your friend, out of loyalty to her. But don't read too much into it. Many men stay on a dating site until they get married—it's sort of a glorified version of porn. They're usually just checking out the pictures, fantasizing, seeing how marketable they still are; it's okay as long as they don't have actual dates. After the wedding, they normally let it go. It's like landing a great job but still keeping your résumé out there with headhunters." —NANCY SLOTNICK, a love-life-management specialist who has consulted for JDate and whose website, Cablight.com, claims to help a woman find the man of her dreams in less than six months

You're looking for the right person, but you're not even sure what the right dating site is. How do you decide among JDate .com, Match.com, Perfectmatch.com, Gay.com, Nerve.com, RightStuffDating.com, eHarmony.com, and TheOnion.com?

"There are basically three kinds of dating sites: free, big, and boutique. Say no to the free ones unless you're doing it just for fun. Big ones like Match.com, which charge a fee, are likely to attract people who are more serious and motivated. People tend to come to boutique sites like JDate and Christian Singles because they really want a serious relationship. Don't give up too quickly. Give it more than a month."
—PEPPER SCHWARTZ, PhD, a relationship expert and the author of numerous books, magazine articles, and website columns, and a television personality on the subject of sexuality

The love of your life likes to Skype, to be able to look into your beautiful eyes. You'd rather talk on the phone so you can multitask. Can you skip the Skype?

"To get out of Skyping, I'd say I'm a hopeless technoturkey so I'd rather talk on the phone. I don't add that this also lets me Google, doodle, e-mail, eat, and change the cat litter at the same time. If you're on-cam, you can't really get away with that." —A REAL ESTATE AGENT whose fiancé travels to South America on business

He's totally macho. He played football in college. You're getting more and more attracted to him as time goes on. Then, in a moment of candor, he tells you that his secret addiction is CuteOverload.com. Is this a deal breaker? A sign of his sweetness and sensitivity? Would a porn website be healthier?

"A great many football players have not only very high levels of testosterone but also high levels of estrogen—associated with empathy, imagination, and linguistic and people skills. So for me, a footballer who loves animals would be a plus. I would probably ask him to marry me." —HELEN FISHER, PhD, an anthropology professor, human behavior researcher, and relationship expert whose current book is titled *Why Him? Why Her?*

"Obviously you've just secured the best of both worlds: a football-playing kitten lover. Sink your teeth in like it's Shark Week and *don't let go!*" —MEG FROST, founder of CuteOverload .com, the warm and fuzzy site that has won numerous awards and been named one of *Time* magazine's 50 Coolest Websites

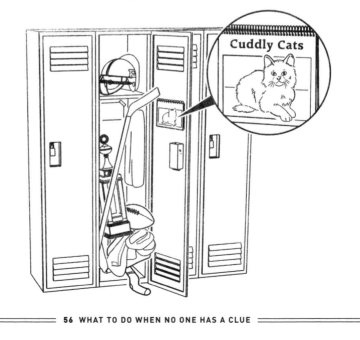

You're moving back home with Mom and Dad to save money. "It's just temporary," you assure them, the person you're dating, and yourself. Where/when/how do you have sex?

"It depends on who Mommy and Daddy are. If you're Pepper Schwartz, no problem! I have a son living with me now—he could marry, have children, and stay with me forever and I'd be happy. Aside from the fact that I'm comfortable with his sexuality, he's in a steady relationship, so there's not a parade of women traipsing in and out. And our bedrooms aren't right next to each other—the physical space is comfortable for all of us. On the other hand, if your parents are conservative, respect their values." —PEPPER SCHWARTZ, PhD, a University of Washington sociologist, the author of fourteen books about relationships, and a sexuality adviser for WebMD

You're looking for True Love. Given the legal troubles and layoffs plaguing the financial industry, are you better off dating the bartender than the banker?

"Only if you'd be happier *marrying* the bartender. The banker who loses a job will eventually have a chance to reinvent him- or herself, so I'd put my money on the banker." —dating coach EVAN MARC KATZ, author of *Why You're Still Single* (Note: He's not) and creator of the online dating system FindingTheOneOnline.com

If you're gay but you were married to a woman and you have two daughters, when do you break this to the guys you are dating?

"I tell them pretty quickly. Everyone responds well to honesty, and there is the assumption that if you are a father, you are nurturing. Frankly, I am more loath to tell the guy I have two cats than two kids." —A FORTY-YEAR-OLD GALLERY OWNER in Portland, Oregon, who has been in this situation more than once

Is a guy who lets a woman pay her own way on a date a modern man . . . or just cheap?

"He's a cheap loser. No self-respecting man, poor or rich, will let a woman pay. It's emasculating. His biology says that *he* takes care of *her*. If he thinks he's going to let her pick up the tab, he better just cut off his penis because he's a sexual eunuch. Bring me a feminist and she's either married to a gay man or she's single." —PATTI STANGER, star of the Bravo TV series *The Millionaire Matchmaker* and author of *Become Your Own Matchmaker*

"A guy who is financially withholding is going to be emotionally withholding as well." —JERILYN KRONEN, PhD, a psychotherapist who counsels couples

Is it okay to blog about the person you are dating?

"Blogging about your date is the virtual equivalent of getting a tattoo with his or her name. It might seem like a great idea when you're happy and in the first blush of love. But even the most perfect relationship has moments of tension. In those less than happy times, the last thing you want to do is read about your partner on the Internet. Unlike a tattoo, things on the Web have a habit of staying there permanently."
—BLOGGER CHERIE BURBACH, the "Dating" feature writer for Suite101.com (she met her husband online) and the author of *Internet Dating Is Not Like Ordering a Pizza*

4

HOW TO

LIVE

WITH YOUR FAMILY

[LOVE 'EM AND/OR
LEAVE 'EM]

Rules are changing. Roles are blending. Genders are blurring. And "family" is anything you make of it. But what can you make of it when these connections are so puzzling? Your new aunt is five years younger than you are and wants you to call her "aunt." Your eighty-five-year-old father announces that he and his twenty-five-year-old housekeeper are expecting. You see your devoted parish priest in a torrid embrace with a parishioner on a beach in Miami. Three of your siblings have book contracts for memoirs chronicling growing up in your dysfunctional family.

We're not at a loss for family. But we *are* at a loss for words. What do you say to the nineteen-year-old nanny who married your ex-husband? Your daughter is dating "Dana" and you can't tell, after you're introduced, whether Dana is her boyfriend or girlfriend. Asked at the wedding how she likes her new stepmother, a Washington advertising executive says, "She's not my stepmother, she's my father's wife." The woman at the cocktail party announces that she's the fourth Mrs. Theodore G. Herzog III.

Family activities abound. But do you really want to sequence your genes, cyberstalk your ex, be buried with your beagle? You can celebrate Mother's Day with your birth mother, the mother who raised you, your stepmother, the surrogate mother of your child, the egg donor, or your ex-mother-in-law. Wouldn't it be simpler to send a card?

Even family fun is a bit iffy. If you want a new way to celebrate some special family moments, you can whip one up with your very own Crawling Zombie Torso Gelatin Mold (ThinkGeek.com), which actually turns out an anatomically correct and wonderfully wobbly gelatin torso. The site says that it's just the thing for holiday parties, retirement parties, children's birthday parties, and even just friendly get-togethers, adding, "Nothing says 'Let's have some calm relaxing fun' or 'Happy 90th Birthday, Grandma—you'll look like this soon' like a Zombie Gelatin Delight. . . . It's delish!" Is this something Grandma would like?

New parenting options are worth celebrating, but do you want to be known as the "helicopter parent" (always hovering), the "idle parent" (who believes that paying attention to parental needs will help their child thrive), or the "placeholder parent" (just there until your child goes to college or gets married)? Can you just bake the cookies, go to the soccer games, and be a parent?

Apparently, it's not as simple as that. Find out how to clear up the confusion with a family of experts, including a marriage counselor, a family therapist, a matrimonial lawyer, a clinical psychologist, a dean of admissions, a mommy blogger, an attorney for the Animal Legal Defense Fund, and a gay father of two daughters. ⇨

Your child's nursery school teacher shows the class a bunch of fresh dill. "What does this make you think of?" she asks. Your son says, "Green." His best friend says, "Gravlax." Do you owe your child a broader worldview?

"Yes, parents owe their kids a more comprehensive exposure to and education about what they are eating. I don't know if that counts as a broader worldview, but it would make kids aware of what they are eating so that they will understand taste and smell." —Robert W. Surles, author of *Chef Bobo's Good Food Cookbook* and former instructor at the French Culinary Institute

Should you be concerned if the top item on your child's birthday wish list is the Playmobil Security Check Point, complete with metal detector, X-ray screening machine, and brightly colored plastic armed officers?

"It might be a useful tool for preparing a child to travel, provided there's plenty of parental interaction and you don't just stick it in the playroom for your child to figure out. But the best toys for young children are open-ended to foster imagination, while a security checkpoint can never be anything else." —Kim Sibley, owner of Little Urbanites in Portland, Oregon, and LittleUrbanites.com; her training in early childhood education informs her store, website, and worldview

You've replaced the screen-saver picture of your five-year-old with a picture of the family's adorable new Labradoodle. What do you say when your child asks, "Where did my picture go?"

"Five-year-olds are just starting to get the idea of permanence. Explain that there are lots of pictures saved in your computer.

That way your child sees that his or her picture isn't 'gone.' And then relax. It's not going to irreparably harm your child if you look at the Labradoodle." —PSYCHOLOGIST ARTHUR ROBIN, PhD, coauthor of *Your Defiant Teen* and chief of psychology at Children's Hospital of Michigan in Detroit

You shell out $400 to take your six- and eight-year-old children to their first Broadway musical and find yourself watching *Avenue Q*'s Sesame Street–style puppets fornicate onstage. Should you pretend they're just dancing?
"Ask the kids to explain what is going on. Their responses may make the $400 investment actually worth it."
—SCHOOL LIBRARIAN LIZ KRIEGER, who's used to encouraging children to read between the lines

What does it say about you if you watch *Supernanny* and feel better when you see that other people's kids are more screwed up than yours?
"It says you're human, and I think it's a natural reaction. We use the show as a gauge. Supernanny Jo Frost is interesting, and you can try to learn from her—you just might not admit it to your friends!" —ELIZABETH THIELE, BusyMom.net blogger and Nashville mother of a seven-year-old, a twelve-year-old, and a fourteen-year-old
    "If the worst thing that's wrong with my kids that day is that they won't eat their spinach, it's not so bad compared with watching someone else's kid about to put the cat in the fireplace. There are no perfect parents." —ANN RYAN, mother of two, who markets educational DVDs for children

Do you need to lie to your kids about everything you did in high school?

"Younger kids want perfect, idealized parents. Later, in their need to separate, they start to see their parents as the most unfair, stupid people on the planet. They will find plenty to complain about no matter what, so pick and choose what ammunition you hand out." —ALEXIS JOHNSON, PhD, family therapist

"I'm pretty honest. I told them that I smoked once in a while. That I experimented with pot. And that I had been drunk at a few parties. But I didn't kill anyone. Until I became a doctor . . . I'm kidding!" —A TOP HOUSTON NEUROSURGEON who has two teenagers and a sense of humor

Your daughter is going to her first prom. You remember enough about your own high school prom to be worried. How can you let her know that you trust her judgment but still keep tabs on her so you know she's safe and sober?

"I'm so grateful for all the technology that made my daughter accountable and even let me grab a few winks of sleep. I had her text me at agreed-upon intervals throughout the night. First, when she was on the bus going to the after-party. Then when the party was over. When she arrived at her friend's house, I had her call me so I could touch base with the friend's mother, too. She texted me when they headed to the beach, and when it was time to drive home, I had her talk to me on her cell the whole time while her friend drove. It was my way of 'being there' to remind them to pay attention because her mother was also paying attention!" —HELAINE, a bond trader who is the mother of three teenage daughters

When do you tell your friends that your dad is gay?

"It tends to come out casually in conversation with a 'Well, my dad's boyfriend' followed by a 'Wait, did you say boyfriend? Okay, that's cool.' From there, if needed, there is a small explanation of things—a shortened version of my life story." —SARAH GWINN, a graphic designer in Washington, D.C.

"When I was in elementary school I used to brag about it as if it were something special. Now I wait until I know someone and feel comfortable telling them. My dad is a major part of my life, so it is hard for me not to talk about him without explaining that he is gay pretty early on. I usually say, 'He came out when I was four; everything is great; I wouldn't have it any other way.'" —TAYLOR GWINN, Sarah's sister, a college student in Virginia

"My response would be: Not until *after* he comes out of the closet." —AUBYN GWINN, Sara and Taylor Gwinn's dad and the design director for a top advertising agency

You are helping your daughter move into her freshman college dorm and notice that the resident adviser on her hall has a box of condoms taped to her door with a sign that says, TAKE ONE. Can you/should you/how can you point this out without mortifying your daughter?

"There is no hope on this one. You might as well make some sort of inappropriate joke that she will be embarrassed by for the rest of her life. When you can joke and be comfortable around sensitive topics, it helps create a healthy outlook on life in our kids and it definitely keeps the communication lines open." —KRISTIN JONES, who attended a university where this was commonplace

Your son opts for the "clothing optional" dorm and you're trying to be cool about it. How do you avoid embarrassing yourself or mortifying your college freshman on move-in day?

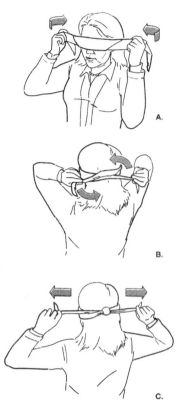

"Wear sunglasses when you are moving stuff into your progeny's dorm room. You want to appear as unruffled about this situation as possible, and looking at naked teenage bodies could ruffle you. Don't tell your friends about this. It will make them question even more the upbringing that you provided your children."

—ROBERT CLAGETT, dean of admissions at Middlebury College

Are you hip and trendy or clingy and pathetic if you buy yourself a second home near the town where your kid goes to college?

"If you do this, you are way too merged with your kids. They need a place of their own. So cancel the real estate agent and send your kids a plane ticket to come home and visit you."

—PSYCHOTHERAPIST PHYLLIS COHEN, CSW

The relationship is *over*. Should you hold on to the jewelry and the memories or cash them in on ExBoyfriendJewelry.com or IDoNowIDont.com?

"Definitely hold on to the jewelry. I don't care one iota about my ex, but I love the emerald earrings and the sapphire bracelet he gave me. I think of him fleetingly when I wear them (which is often). The only time it felt slightly odd was when I wore the earrings on a date with his friend. (Don't ask.)" —ANGELA FIORI, a twenty-seven-year-old whose ex-boyfriend's father was a jeweler

"Keep it! I decided that diamonds have the ability to slough off any bad memories associated with them. If the memories are *too* strong, take the stones and reset them. That also 'resets' their history!" —A WELL-ACCESSORIZED WOMAN who's been divorced for several years

You divorce your husband but, for your daughter's sake, keep his name so that yours matches hers. A year later, she gets married and drops his name. Are you stuck with it forever?

"Absolutely not. Your only problem is deciding what name you want to go by: your birth name (that is, your father's), your new name (should that happen), or one you create, confounding future generations as to who you really were and how you fit into the family tree." —A CLINICAL PSYCHOLOGIST and family therapist in Atlanta

"While my daughter changed her name, I still kept my married name but merged it with my maiden name. I figured that I spent the same number of years with each name, so the person I am today is a combination of the two. But if I had it to do over, I wouldn't have changed my name when I married—

not to prepare for a potential divorce but because we would have started the marriage on equal footing."

—DIANE JASS KETELHUT, PhD, a professor and mother of two

Your ex, who hasn't spoken to you or responded to an e-mail in three years, asks you to be a friend on Facebook. What's your response?

"Three solutions:

1. Respond by saying that your e-mail relationship is enough. (Don't even acknowledge that you don't have one.)
2. Take it as an invitation to write on his wall what you've been dying to get off your chest for the last three years.
3. Don't try to make sense of someone who didn't make much sense for fifteen years."

—A LOS ANGELES MARRIAGE COUNSELOR

HEARTLESS, CLUELESS, KIDNEYLESS

After four years of divorce proceedings and weary of the battle, Long Island, New York, surgeon Richard Batista demanded that his estranged wife return the kidney he donated to her. Or, he added, he'd settle for $1.5 million in compensation. Manhattan attorney Susan Moss assessed his odds on Law.com: "The good doctor is out of luck and out a kidney."

You have two tickets for your child's graduation and there are three parents. What do you do?

"First, find out if any of your son's or daughter's friends' parents won't be needing both of their tickets. Then, if necessary, *beg* a college administrator to find an extra ticket (they can usually find one somewhere). If that doesn't work, give the two tickets to your roommate's family and have all three parents watch the ceremony on the wide-screen TV in the student center." —ROBERT CLAGETT, dean of admissions at Middlebury College

You discover—by accident—that your divorce lawyer is in the middle of her own messy divorce and is having trouble concentrating on yours. Should you divorce her?

"Yes. If she is having trouble concentrating on your case, for whatever reason, then you need a lawyer who can. We are all human and have our own problems, so some understanding and flexibility is appropriate—such as if your lawyer has a death in the family or an illness of limited duration. But the example posed would make me worry that you would not have your counsel's complete attention for an uncertain and potentially lengthy amount of time. Also, since a divorce is such an emotionally wrenching experience, your counsel may lose her objectivity on your case by relating it to her own."

—ALLAN MAYEFSKY, a partner in the law firm of Sheresky Aronson Mayefsky & Sloan and the president of the New York State chapter of the American Academy of Matrimonial Lawyers

Larry and Jacob are getting married. Is it TMI for the announcement to include the fact that "Mr. Jones's first marriage ended in divorce, as did Mr. Smith's"—when clearly (given how recent legal gay marriage is) those first marriages were to women?

"Why would anyone want to announce to the world they were a failure at something—in this case, being a straight man? Or that they couldn't figure out that they were gay till well into adulthood?" —Robert George, who wed his longtime partner during the brief window when California legalized gay marriage

If you can't get to a cousin's funeral, should you ask if the funeral will be webcast so you can "be there" with the family at their time of grief?
"Some people are not comfortable with anything electronic, and we need to respect that. However, if the choice is for someone to be able to participate in a service hours, or even days, afterward because of the impossibility of attending, it has tremendous value. I can only relate the thanks we have received from all over the world from people who otherwise would have not been able to see or hear a service at all and would have felt very left out." —John Carmon, past president of the National Funeral Directors Association and owner of Carmon Community Funeral Homes in Windsor, Connecticut, an early adopter of funeral webcasting technology

Are you bitter, vindictive, or just moving on when you Photoshop your ex out of the family photos?
"It doesn't make any difference if it makes you feel better. Just keep the family intact on the mantel, if nowhere else."
—a psychotherapist and marriage counselor in Washington, D.C.

From the beginning, you both loved him, babied him, laughed at how adorable he was, and gave him everything he needed to grow up big and healthy and happy. So who gets the dog and/or the dog's ashes in the divorce?

"It's always better to deal with this issue up front, in writing, even though you think and hope it will never be an issue. These days, more and more courts will enforce a pet prenuptial agreement. Otherwise people may end up spending thousands of dollars for the court to determine who was the legal owner of the dog during its lifetime. Some couples have actually divided up the ashes into two urns. Others alternate custody of their beloved's remains, but this can get nasty. I know of one case where the ex was accused of swapping out the ashes with fireplace ashes." —ATTORNEY LISA McCURDY, an associate at Schiff Hardin in San Francisco, which represents the Animal Legal Defense Fund

You want to nominate your sister for one of the style makeover shows on TV. Will she be eternally grateful to you for helping her give up those mauve jogging suits and the striped leg warmers? Or will she (should she) hate you forever?

"Your sister will probably thank you for doing this, and remember, she won't go on the show if she doesn't want to. If she gets upset because you nominated her, point out the following:

1. You simply signed her up to have free consultations with experts, and then get many thousands of dollars with which to buy stuff. How could that ever be a bad thing?

2. Like it or not, we live in a world that judges by physical appearance. Is it so bad to want the world to realize her excellence the minute they meet her, instead of after they've known her long enough to look past the sweatpants and the wretched cat sweater?

3. If your siblings aren't allowed to tell you you have terrible style, who is, really?"

—A FASHIONISTA who grew up worshipping at the shrine of Anna Wintour

"Frankly, you're better off having a sister who hates you forever than a sister with bad fashion sense."

—A CLEARHEADED WOMAN who always looks fabulous and hasn't paid retail since she was thirteen

HOMER GOES POSTAL

In response to the United States Postal Service's announcement that it would issue stamps honoring *The Simpsons* (Homer, Marge, Bart, Lisa, and Maggie each get a stamp), James L. Brooks, executive producer of the show, said, "We are emotionally moved by the Postal Service selecting us rather than making the lazy choice of someone who has benefited society."

You stop by the Nars counter and the saleswoman persuades your conservative mother to try a new lip gloss. She loves the color and asks the name. "Orgasm," the saleswoman announces. Smiling sweetly at your mother, she adds, "Everyone loves it." Do you buy it? Laugh? Quickly ask you mother where she'd like to go to lunch?

"You have to make a joke out of it. Say, 'They don't name them like they used to!' And who knows, it might turn into an unexpected moment to bond with your mother."

—ELAINE D'FARLEY, beauty director of a major women's magazine

5

HOW TO

HAVE
BABIES

[MOTHERS AND OTHERS]

You can't conceive of all the decisions that are required from the moment of conception to the day the indulged adolescent starts referring to his or her parents as "two in help."

First, there's the decision about a name. Or perhaps a title. One thing you know, right off the bat, is that you do not want to follow in Jermaine Jackson's steps and name your child "Jermajesty." Will this confused child think he is royalty and insist on issuing decrees to all of his subjects? When he gets older, will he look for dragons to slay in Brentwood and ask Queen Elizabeth if he can be her Facebook friend?

There is also the decision about what to give the new parents. Forget silver helium balloons or a home-baked lemon-glazed pound cake. TheRecoveryKit.com offers childbirth and C-section healing gift kits from chic C-section underwear to a personal chef to camouflage makeup. The company's slogan is "Bringing you back . . . with style," which suggests not only that the new mother might be dead tired but that at some point she was actually dead.

There are decisions about toys: What to give the gifted child? Do you go fun or green? You can choose a plastic Big Lebowski bobblehead, but doesn't your little tree hugger deserve a stimulating eco-toy like the Discovery Paper Recycling Studio? Or a toy recycling truck by Green Toys that's made from recycled milk jugs?

There are decisions you'll face based on all the questions that come up—but don't go online unless you are prepared for some tough ones. BabyZone.com asks, "Are you and your baby an astrological match?" On ABCNews.go.com, *Good Morning America* asks, "Do you love, but not like, your child?" Babies

Today.com queries, "Can exercise make your baby smarter?" ParentDish.com asks, "Would you drug your child to enhance academic performance?" IVillage.com asks, "Does your child have an accent?" At least About.com provides solid advice about the challenge all parents will face sooner or later: "How to Keep Your Teen from Becoming an Online Porn Star." Whatever child-rearing doubts and fears you have, happily, there's always someone to give you more. Free!

Then there are decisions thrust upon us by evolving technology: How do you explain "the birds and the bees" to a child who was conceived through IVF? When you're choosing a child-care center, will your toddler stay healthier if you pick one with hands-free sensor-activated bathroom faucets? ("Must-have technology," says Forbes.com.) What do you say when your phone bill shows that your teenager has sent more than $4,000 in text messages in one month?

Although your children will still blame you for everything you do (or neglect to do), experts to help you minimize the damage include a leading authority on baby names, the founder of BabymoonFinders.com, a gynecologist, psychologists who specialize in defiant teens and lesbian parenting, and the mother of an adopted baby born in China. ⇨

Rick (gay) is the stepuncle to Rebecca (a lesbian). Rebecca and her partner want a baby. They choose Rick's partner, Jonathan, to supply the sperm. What do we call Jonathan: the father, the sperm donor, a stepuncle, or something else?

"I've had two similar experiences with family. In one, the lesbian couple wanted to call my brother 'uncle,' and that, combined with the level of attachment they kept implying, made my brother eventually decline. He wanted to be a donor, not an uncle. In the other, the folks are all close, the donor provides child care, and they are all friends, but there's no title for the donor. He's just 'Jonathan.' I would like to add that I think the child should know where he or she came from. It is just that saying, 'The sperm donor is coming over for dinner tonight' is kinda weird."—MANGUS, a participant in the online community Fluther.com

Is it overkill to take a $1,000 "babymoon" at a luxury hotel when it's going to cost you $418,702 to raise a child from infancy to college?

"Our generation wants to truly be pampered before the Pampers. The average costs for a babymoon at an all-inclusive spa resort can run up to $4,000 or more, which can be daunting, especially if your income will drop or vanish during maternity leave. For couples on a budget—like we were—it's fun to stay in your hometown and indulge in a 'pregnancy package' offered by a local spa, or take a couples massage class." —ASHLEY KING, founder of BabymoonFinder.com, which offers hundreds of prebaby getaways all over the world

DIRECT DEPOSIT?

Lisa and Lori had a child together through a sperm donor. When their son reached nursery school and was figuring out mommies and daddies, he asked about his own daddy. The two moms told him that his daddy "came from the sperm bank." From then on, whenever one of his moms said she was going to the bank, the child would excitedly say, "You'll see my daddy!"

Is it okay to ask a lesbian how she got pregnant?

"We haven't landed on our feet yet in this fertile new world. Bottom line: It depends on why you're asking. If you see a stranger in the supermarket, don't ask. It could come across as a prurient question. But if it's a colleague whom you're close to and you want to be supportive, it could be very appropriate to ask. My husband and I are Caucasian. Our baby granddaughter is biracial and a lovely chocolate brown. One day we were walking down the street with her and a little boy screeched to a stop on his bicycle and asked, 'How'd you do that?' It's all about trying to make sense of the universe."
—DIANE EHRENSAFT, PhD, a developmental and clinical psychologist in the San Francisco Bay Area and the author of *Mommies, Daddies, Donors, Surrogates*

"If you know her well enough, go ahead. But realize that it's not a question people ask heterosexual women. So it can be stigmatizing." —G. DORSEY GREEN, PhD, a Seattle-based psychologist and a coauthor, with D. Merilee Clunis, PhD, of *The Lesbian Parenting Book*

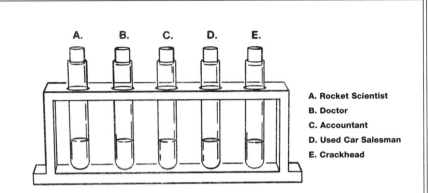

A. Rocket Scientist
B. Doctor
C. Accountant
D. Used Car Salesman
E. Crackhead

When you're considering artificial insemination, is it worth it to pay more for the sperm of an Ivy League PhD candidate? And would this mean that the kid can say he or she is a legacy at Harvard?

"If a PhD is important to you, then yes, pay extra for it. If it is in your budget to get photographs of the donor (once you have decided he has all or most of the other qualities on your list), definitely get them—the more information the better."

—Tracy, a thirty-seven-year-old Portland, Oregon, mother of a toddler with her wife, Sue

"It may be worth it to pay for the attributes that can be measured, like educational achievement and appearance. But you need to keep in mind that other important attributes can't be measured, like decency, kindness, and temperament. And you don't know which combination of genes the baby will actually get." —a psychiatrist in private practice

Your friend pulls out six sonograms of her grandchild-to-be. They are dark and murky, remind you of seventh-grade biology, and look like every other sonogram you've ever seen. Your friend is beaming and waiting for your response. Your response?

"'Oh wow, look at that—simply amazing, our technology, no?' Then tell her she should post it on Facebook so she can 'tag' her future child and create his or her profile ahead of time. (The baby will start out with many, many more friends in life this way.)" —A QUICK-THINKING MOTHER of two

All four doting grandparents-to-be, along with the mother-to-be's sister, sister-in-law, and best friend, have insisted that they be the very first to know the minute the couple learns whether it's a boy or girl. So whom do they call first?
"My son and daughter-in-law are setting up a conference call, giving each of us a password and a phone number to call at exactly nine P.M. on the day they get the results."
—AN EXPECTANT GRANDMOTHER who is waiting to see whether she should think pink or think blue

Lisa Bonet named her baby Nakoa-Wolf Manakauapo Namakaeha Momoa. Gwyneth Paltrow has Apple. Nicole Kidman has Sunday. Ashlee Simpson has Bronx Mowgli. Is it okay not to name your baby after a Hawaiian princess, a fruit, a day, a place? Is Jane such a bad idea?
"Parents feel a lot of pressure to choose the perfect name for their baby. As much as you might not like this idea, a name is part of a child's 'brand,' and people will react to it the way they might to the name of a car or a candy bar: 'Oh, that's cool'—or 'modern' or 'dumb' or 'girly.' You need to be conscious of issues like what image the name carries and whether that's in line with what you want for your child. But in the end, you might choose to set all those weighty consid-

WHAT'S IN A NAME?

After going through three what-to-name-the-baby books, a young couple in Marblehead, Massachusetts, came to the conclusion that their favorite name for their daughter-to-be was one they had already given to their cat: Hazel. They then realized that if their cat and their child were both named Hazel, people would be likely to conclude that they were—even before the baby was born—incredibly lazy and uncreative parents. Not to mention thoughtless about the trauma this could cause their beloved pet. So they named the baby Hazel and changed the cat's name to "Mr. Baseball," which he liked better anyway, since he is a boy. They never bothered to change the pet-tag name on his collar, since neither he nor baby Hazel could read.

erations aside and just pick a name you like, whether it's Java or Jane."
—PAMELA REDMOND SATRAN, coauthor of *Beyond Ava and Aiden, The Baby Name Bible,* and *Cool Names for Babies,* and cofounder of the online baby-name database Nameberry.com (as well as the mother of Rory, Joe, and Owen)

You're on the street and a passerby stops to admire your six-month-old twins. After finding out that one baby is a girl and the other a boy, this inquisitive woman asks you, "Are they identical?" Your response?
"Yes. Except for the penis." —ANDREA SCOTTING, a Brooklyn mother of twins, who gets this question a lot

The pregnant woman's sister is a doula. Her best friend is a midwife. The mom-to-be wants her baby born in a hospital, and she wants an epidural. She doesn't think her child will care that she didn't give birth in a kiddie pool or sitting on a bouncy ball. What should she/can she say to her sister and best friend?

"Both midwives and doulas emphasize that a woman should have her baby where she is most comfortable. Their assumption is that she will feel most comfortable at home. My sister and my friend understood that for me, a hospital was the most comfortable and natural place. There's no reason anyone should be judgmental, and there doesn't need to be a clash. Oh—and they bought me a bouncy ball anyway!"
—A TWENTY-SIX-YEAR-OLD WOMAN who was in this position and chose to give birth at a hospital

Should a pregnant woman ask her parents or best friend to be with her in the delivery room when the baby is born? Can she change her mind halfway through?

"My mother was there when I had my third child—I was older and more comfortable with the idea by then. And so was she. We bonded intensely because she shared in the birth, but then after about ten minutes, things went back to normal—warm and loving with the occasional mother/daughter complication." —CYNTHIA KRAUSE, MD, assistant clinical professor of gynecology, Mount Sinai Hospital, and mother of three

You adopted a baby from China. The first time you bring her to your parents' country club, one of their friends says, "What a sweetheart! How much did she cost?" And your response?

"'Aren't all children just priceless?' I've been asked that question at least half a dozen times. These other gems have come, surprisingly, from friends and relatives and people you'd think would know better: 'Do you think she'll have an affinity for Chinese food?' (This from someone who's a member of Mensa.) 'What language will she be speaking when you bring her home?' (The baby was ten months old then.) And the conversation-stopping 'Do you think she realizes she's Oriental?'" —MICHELLE, the mother of a daughter who was born in China

TOT TEES. BIG TROUBLE.

It used to be that babies couldn't talk, but thanks to an endlessly "creative" selection of tiny T-shirts with slogans, now even your one-month-old can say a mouthful. A few examples:

"I only cry when ugly people hold me"

"Boobs for dinner"

"Another fine product of a dysfunctional family"

"My daddy's a lawyer, but I still love him"

"My dad's a freak. Fo'shizzle"

"My mother doesn't want your advice"

"Someday I'll get trashed at the prom"

And this, the all-time low:

"All Daddy wanted was a blow job"

Of course, the babies displaying these slogans must have a dad who is wearing a T-shirt that says, "Your trailer park called. Their trash is missing" and a mom who is sporting "I'm not a proctologist, but I know an asshole when I see one."

A colleague just back from maternity leave pulls out graphic photographs of the birth. Do you have to look?

"No, you don't have to look. But you have a few options that might clue her in to just how inappropriate that is. Tell her you have some pictures of your hemorrhoid procedure and ask if she wants to swap. Or ask if she has pictures of the conception to share. Better yet, say 'I'm kind of busy right now. Can you just put them on Flickr and send me a link?'"

—A THIRTY-SEVEN-YEAR-OLD GRAPHIC DESIGNER who works in a large firm and finds the whole idea way too, well, graphic

Your daughter has just given birth and is having trouble breast-feeding. At a family dinner celebrating the new arrival, everybody from grandparents to uncles feels free to discuss her cracked nipples, her recent engorgement, and her new modesty shawl for breast-feeding, called a "Hooter Hider." How do you shift the spotlight off your humiliated daughter and back to the brisket?

"Run interference. Interrupt the conversation by saying something like 'Wow, look at the expression on the baby's face—isn't it so adorable?!' Another solution is for your daughter to say something when she's had enough. A simple 'Thanks for your concern. I've got this thing under control' will do. She might also add, 'And could you pass the gravy?'"

—A WISCONSIN PSYCHOLOGIST whose specialty is counseling new parents

Two young parents across the aisle from you on the plane are holding a crimson-faced baby who is crying and crying and crying. You want to suggest that perhaps it is an ear-pressure problem and that the couple might relieve the pressure by giving their baby a bottle or breast-feeding him. Should you say something?

"On takeoffs and landings, it does work to give the baby something to suck on. And yes, I would say something but only if it was clear that I was concerned. Don't be critical, and do tell them that they're handling it really well. Oh, if there is liquor on the plane and it's after nine A.M., you might want to buy the parents a glass of wine!" —AN EMPATHETIC MOTHER of seventeen-year-old twins

The mother of your son's preschool friend e-mails you a message from her child to pass along to yours. She explains that her child likes to e-mail, so she "translates" her four-year-old's gibberish into the intended message: "slfjfflhjkkkleesizz (Hi, Sam!) eeeehtlbbskkslbiondlkf (I played with blocks today.) Ubltisrebl;ghaowpenhci (My favorite color is orange.)" How do you respond?

"I answered once, thinking it would go away. And the next thing I knew I was in this insane e-mail relationship with an adorable illiterate and an overly involved mom. Note to self: No good deed goes unpunished." —THE MONTESSORI MOTHER who received these e-mails

You're appalled to see your sister-in-law giving her toddler little sips of her wine. Should you say something or vent your feelings on UrbanBaby.com?

"Giving advice on how to raise a kid is a bold way to go for someone who isn't a mother-in-law. It can cause a rift that will last until somebody dies. There are some things that are worth that kind of ill will, but this isn't one of them. Assuming that the sister-in-law is not a raving drunk, she's probably attempting to demystify wine, so her kid grows up like those European teens who have wine with dinner and then don't feel the need to do beer funnels as soon as they hit college. And who knows, maybe she's right. Even if she's wrong, she won't appreciate your saying so. Unless you're protecting a family member from certain, imminent harm, as they say on UrbanBaby, STFU and MYOB." —JOYCE SLATON, editor of UrbanBaby San Francisco and the mother of a four-year-old

You're watching TV when a Viagra commercial comes on, ending with a long list of side effects. Your seven-year-old son turns to you and asks, "What's a four-hour erection?" "Explain what an erection is in very simple terms—when a boy's penis stands up straight. All little boys have experienced this, and it's okay for girls to hear that this happens, too. And then I would emphasize that the four-hour version happens only when certain medicines are taken." —LEONA JAGLOM, PhD, a clinical child psychologist in Brooklyn, New York

Nannycams: How do you find out what you want to know without making yourself crazy? "If you are thinking about a nannycam, get another nanny." —KRISTEN KREBS, a former marketing executive and the mother of two young children who's employed a wonderful nanny for four years

Are you a better parent or a control freak if you opt for a device that tracks how your teenager drives, texts you alerts about where he or she is going, gives you the homework assignments, and tells you what he or she ate for lunch? "The goal of adolescence is to become more independent. Too much parental monitoring means endless arguments and rebellion. Too little, and teens will do whatever they want. Monitoring makes sense earlier in adolescence, with the parent gradually releasing oversight as the teen takes on more responsibility. For a twelve-year-old, I'd check the school website for each night's homework assignment. Hopefully you won't need to do this very often by the time he or she is

seventeen. But if teenagers have ADHD or other issues, you should use all available practical, legal, and moral methods to impose structure for the children who can't do it themselves."
—PSYCHOLOGIST ARTHUR ROBIN, PhD, coauthor of *Your Defiant Teen* and chief of psychology at Children's Hospital of Michigan in Detroit

"Remember that for every device that can be invented, there is a teen who can and will outwit it." —A MOTHER who has gotten two children safely past the teen years

6

HOW TO

EAT
AND DRINK
[PUTTING IT
ON THE TABLE]

You can baffle the chef: "I'm a quasi pesca-vegan." The chef can baffle you: "I suggest the sea urchin ravioli with mango jelly, a fennel jus, and aromatic herbal raspberry foam." The plat du jour is the "inverted Andante Dairy goat cheese and black olive tart with vadovan gastrique, preserved lemon, and wild arugula." (Didn't you rent a Vadovan when you took that camping trip to Belgium?)

Or you can just be baffled. Especially if you are trying to understand why your Brit chum can't stop raving about the Cajun Squirrel flavor chips he fancies. Is he kidding? *Squirrel?* (From Walkers.co.uk.) You *get* poetry slams, but *tofu* slams? And *pork-offs?*

Along with the new flavors and food trends to keep up with, there are new culinary terms and theories. Chefs can be "deconstructivists," food can be "techno-emotional," and to eat cheaply but well, we practice "bistronomics." Forget the parsley—chefs now use methyl cellulose to create signature touches like "magenta films of 'hibiscus paper.'" (Yum!) The rest of the time, it's back to nature, think local, and worship heirloom tomatoes.

Naturally, you're confused. You're not sure what a locavore is. Or whether you want your gin and tonic served as a foam in an egg cup. A woman you meet at the farmers' market tells you that she is a vegetable-rights activist. Is someone denying carrots their rights?

If the politics behind putting dinner on the table aren't

enough to deal with, contending with the knowledge of what's actually in our food is another issue. Does the online review describing the burger you're about to eat as "a La Frieda mix of 25% deckle, 75% chuck, with a lean to fat ratio of 73/27" mean it's going to taste better? Cost more? Be something you could eat in front of Eric Schlosser, author of *Fast Food Nation,* or Morgan *Super Size Me* Spurlock?

The same goes for wine. Do we really need to know that the core flavors—according to a $12 million study—of New Zealand's sauvignon blanc are passion fruit, asparagus, and cat pee? (And couldn't that $12 million have been better spent taking care of stray cats?)

When you're not looking for a new white wine to drink, you're feeling guilty. What's more heinous: eating overfished fish, eating too much salt, eating the wrong kind of salt, shopping in the middle of the supermarket, or not having read Michael Pollan's latest book, even though you lied and said you did?

You will find palatable solutions to today's culinary conundrums from a restaurateur, a cookbook author, a celebrity chef, the star of a TV reality show who's a bestselling author and natural-foods chef, the founding editor of *Saveur* magazine, a caterer to the stars, a committed vegetarian, and an unrepentant carnivore. ⇨

Are you a pain in the ass when you have a special request (excluding any major food allergies) or ask for special treatment in a restaurant? And how does that play out when you are in a restaurant that offers only one menu at dinner?
"It's kind of a toss-up. You want customers to be comfortable, but a lot of customers can be very demanding, acting like they're in someone's house. Regulars who are well loved by the staff get special treatment because they're a part of our family. Of course we try to accommodate food allergies—often we get the news ahead of time in an e-mail. And while we have one set menu at Chez Panisse, we offer a vegetarian option. As to what's a pain: a table full of whims and entitlement and preconceived notions. My feeling is, you're in a good restaurant, so try to be open—you might actually discover you like fava beans or sweetbreads." —DAVID TANIS, head chef at Chez Panisse and author of *A Platter of Figs*

The diner next to you has ordered swordfish—a bad choice, since you know it is overfished. Do you say something to him or her?
"No, that's intrusive. It's really the responsibility of the restaurant not to serve it. So speak to the general manager and let him or her know what you think." —A FOOD WRITER who is on the board of the James Beard Foundation

How do you throw a dinner party when Joe won't touch anything with sugar, Sean and Sara don't eat anything white, Anna is lactose intolerant, and you're starting to feel guest intolerant?

"If you care enough to cater to individual needs, ask in advance. If you don't, offer a variety of foods served family-style, with and without meat and dairy products. Decide that whatever you really like is bound to stir up someone's hidden intolerance—and yours—so go with what's easy, presentable, and cheap." —CORBY KUMMER, author of *The Pleasures of Slow Food* and *The Joy of Coffee* and head of the food section of TheAtlantic.com

"Find some new friends who know how to have fun." —BETHENNY FRANKEL, bestselling author of *Naturally Thin: Unleash Your Skinnygirl* and star of the Bravo TV series *The Real Housewives of New York City*

Is it politically incorrect to eat veal, Chilean sea bass, or foie gras, if given the chance, at a business dinner with clients?
"I'm almost a vegetarian and I have a daughter who has devoted her life to animal rescue, so I'd simply say, 'I don't eat _____' and let them figure out why." —DONNA WARNER, editor in chief, *Metropolitan Home* magazine, and a former food writer who feels sorry for those Chilean sea bass, worse yet for the geese

NO PARSNIP LEFT BEHIND

As a sign of its growing acceptance of diversity, the European Union has relaxed its strict rule that all fruits and vegetables be of uniform size and shape. "This marks a new dawn for the curvy cucumber and the knobbly carrot," announced Mariann Fischer Boel, European commissioner for agriculture.

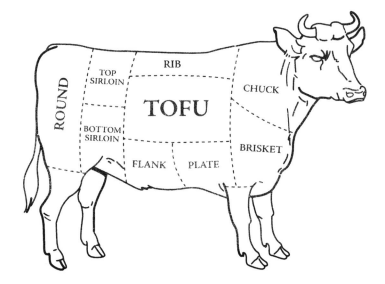

You are a committed vegan and you are invited by a client to a company dinner at a steak house. What should you do?

"I've been a vegetarian since I was four, although it took a year or two after that for me to figure out that hot dogs, chicken nuggets, et cetera, were meat. Here's what I think a vegan should do: Politely accept the invitation and then look up the steak house's menu online to see if there are any items you'd be okay with ordering. If there isn't anything on the menu (or if the menu isn't online), call the restaurant and ask if they would be able to specially prepare any dishes to meet your needs. Chances are, they'll be able to fix you a vegetable plate or pasta, or at the very least a salad." —ANNA DANZIGER, a research assistant at a Washington, D.C., economic and social policy research think tank

You wow your dinner guests with the authentic Spanish gazpacho you bought at the local gourmet shop but served in your fine china soup tureen. One woman is so dazzled that she insists she's not leaving the table without that recipe.
From the catered to: "I'd say that I'm usually very generous with my recipes, but this one is a carefully guarded family secret that I'm not allowed to share. Then I'd ask if she'd like a little more gazpacho." —RUTH HIRSCH, who has been giving memorable (and effortless) dinner parties for more than sixty years
From the caterer: "It's okay to serve the soup with pride. It's also okay to say that you didn't make it yourself and tell the guest where you got it. Look at it this way: Anyone can make bad gazpacho. You had the wisdom to go out and buy a good one!" —ARI WEINZWEIG, cofounding partner of the Zingerman's Community of Businesses in Ann Arbor, Michigan, which includes a million-dollar-plus catering business

The food costs a fortune at a four-star restaurant. And you've got leftovers. Is it gauche to ask to take them home?
"No! Ask and you shall receive. We have earth-friendly packaging just for this occasion at our four-star Topolobampo. We would rather see it go home and be eaten!" —RICK BAYLESS, chef and owner of Frontera Grill and Topolobampo, host of PBS's *Mexico: One Plate at a Time,* and winner of Bravo TV's *Top Chef Masters* competition
        "Who else will be cooking for you as well as these people?" —A FOOD WRITER AND EDITOR who spends a great deal of time in restaurants

MY PINOT NOIR IS A PISCES?

U.K. wine sellers, declaring that wine has horoscopes, have advised wine drinkers to avoid wine on certain days of the month because its taste changes with the lunar cycle. U.K. retailers like Tesco and Marks & Spencer, which sell about a third of all wine drunk in Britain, now invite critics to taste their ranges only at times when the biodynamic calendar suggests they will show at their best.

You ask for a glass of a nice, full-bodied red wine. The waiter suggests a California pinot noir. It is delicious until you get the bill: $26 per glass. Can you lodge a complaint afterward because the waiter should have told you it was so expensive?

"Yes, you can speak up. And should. Part of a waiter's or sommelier's job is to build a relationship with the customer. So when suggesting a wine, he or she always should add a disclaimer like 'A glass costs twenty-six dollars but I think it's phenomenal.' It's a courtesy." —MICHAEL BOTTIGLIERO, wine expert at Chicago's Eno Wine Room

Does it spoil the experience if you or your friends check the menu online ahead of time and decide what to have before you reach the restaurant?

"It only spoils the experience if someone admits it. Stealth and secrecy are required to maintain that fun feeling of group discovery. Being a foodie, I love to study the menu online at length. I am notorious for wanting entrée A but with the sauce from entrée B . . . so knowing what I want ahead of time makes it much less agonizing for my tablemates. To avoid suspicion, I make sure to spend an appropriate amount of time with the menu and offer spontaneous-sounding observations like 'Oh, look—they have poblano corn chowder with crab today!'" —A Napa restaurant regular

You're having brunch with three of your friends at a busy neighborhood bistro. When it comes time to pay the bill, you all put your credit cards on the table and ask the waiter to divide it by four. Is that too much to ask? Is there some rule of thumb about how many credit cards you can give?

"It's definitely not too much to ask. We're completely customer-focused, so we'll take as many credit cards as you want to give. Of course, if it's a quick pretheater dinner and you've got to get out in a hurry, that might not be the best time to give us ten credit cards!" —Ari Weinzweig of the much-loved foodie destination Zingerman's Roadhouse in Ann Arbor, Michigan

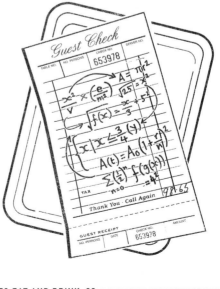

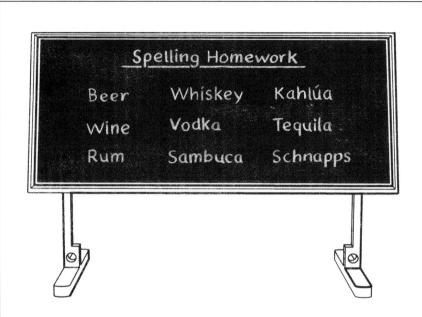

Spelling Homework

Beer   Whiskey   Kahlúa

Wine   Vodka   Tequila

Rum   Sambuca   Schnapps

Your family is having dinner in a neighborhood restaurant that advertises bargain-priced martinis for teachers on Tuesdays. Wait—isn't that your child's second-grade teacher ordering her third Teacher-Tini? Will she be happier if you go over and say hi or if you don't?

"We tend to hold teachers to a higher standard, but that's not always fair. They're people, too. Our blog has stories about questionable teachers coming to school drunk, or going out drinking with their students. But as long as the teacher isn't out drinking with *your* kid, just go up and say hi. If it's obvious that he or she is not firing on all cylinders, simply steer the kids away to avoid embarrassing someone. Of course, if I were the student, I'd be shooting cell phone videos and putting them up on YouTube . . ." —Anthony David Adams, cofounder of the education blog DetentionSlip.org

You're at a top restaurant whose chef is renowned for her pitch-perfect dishes. The waitstaff tells you that the chef recommends cooking something medium rare, but you want it well done. What do you do?

"Anytime you have the chance—and the money—to try a great chef's food, it's worth experiencing his work in the form he intends. So if the dish is part of a tasting menu, ask for a substitution, and if you're ordering à la carte, pick a different dish!" —CELIA BARBOUR, contributing editor at *O* magazine and a former writer for the *New York Times'* "Dining In" column

"Of course I have reasons for why I cook something a certain way and am always happy to explain. For example: Venison is way too lean to taste good when it is well-done. I hate having to ruin a perfectly good piece of meat, but the bottom line is that we are in the hospitality business, so we will do what a diner asks." —ANITA LO, chef and co-owner of the New York restaurant Annisa and a finalist on Bravo TV's *Top Chef Masters*

You are in a restaurant in Napa. The server asks, "Would you like some of our specially purified water?" You don't want to appear gauche, or stupid, or anti-green. Do you ask about the provenance? The price? Or just say, "We'll have the tap water"?

"Some people do get flustered and ask for tap water right away. But our servers are happy to explain why we only serve our own purified water. It's pure and healthy, and it tastes great. My advice is to ask anything you want about anything on the menu. Everyone loves foodies with questions. And, honestly, a healthy dialogue makes the dining experience more fun and satisfying for everyone." —RICH POLIAK, owner of Elements Restaurant & Enoteca (whose very Napa business card reads: "Head Foodie & Wine Geek")

"The more interesting moment is the 'sparkling or still' moment. Always answer 'club soda from the gun' so they don't try to clip you on the $8 bottle of sparkling water. Club soda with lime is green and just as good."

—BETHENNY FRANKEL, bestselling author of *Naturally Thin: Unleash Your Skinnygirl* and star of the Bravo TV series *The Real Housewives of New York City*

You're having lunch with three coworkers at a seafood restaurant near your office. The pregnant coworker is thinking of sashimi. The office manager is about to order farmed salmon. The admin is going for the orange roughy. You want to order them all to go online immediately to TipthePlanet.com or SustainableFishery.com. What, if anything, do you say?

"I'd feel a moral obligation to speak up. They need to know about species that are endangered, fish full of parasites and PCBs, and dangerously high mercury levels! I'd say something like 'Maybe so-and-so would be a better choice.' And I might add how confusing it is these days for any of us to know what we can or should eat—things change weekly. And next time we went out to eat, I'd suggest an Italian restaurant!"

—NANCY STEPHENS, who is on the executive board of directors of the Union of Concerned Scientists

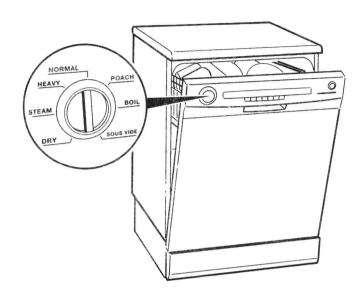

Your overzealous eco-conscious friend invites you to dinner. The main course is a salmon he poached in the dishwasher to cut down on carbon emissions. Your reaction?

"Just shoot me. Oh, please. It's like putting your cat in the washing machine. No guest should ever be presented with salmon cooked that way. The great thing about being green is how truly simple it is: prize the ingredients. Don't do very much to them. Serve them." —AN AWARD-WINNING COOKBOOK AUTHOR AND EDITOR

To impress you, your date takes you to a four-star restaurant and orders the satsuma with a clove and Sauternes sauce, followed by the Nantucket bay scallops with uni crème, ama ebi, and Marcona almonds. Can you just order the roast chicken?

"Absolutely. If it's on the menu, go for it. There's nothing better than a perfect roast chicken. Choose what you want and don't be embarrassed. If your date is snarky about it—well, you shouldn't be going out with that kind of food snob."

—Sara Moulton, cookbook author and TV host, former chef at *Gourmet* magazine's executive dining room, and food editor at *Good Morning America*

Your significant other is a vegetarian. You're not, although you prepare meatless meals when you're cooking for the two of you. One day your sweetheart asks how, if you really love animals (you've rescued two dogs and three cats), you can justify eating meat. How do you answer?

"It's easy. When someone is that dogmatic, my suggestion is, don't give up the meat; give up the non–meat eater."

—a twenty-eight-year-old carnivore who lives with a menagerie of shelter animals and once drove 150 miles to rescue a rabbit

How do you (*or do you?*) let your hostess know that you're carbophobic and your partner is allergic to crustaceans and porcini mushrooms?

"Never lead with allergies or phobias. Don't make it an issue. If I go someplace and the main dish is lobster, my husband and I just say, 'Can you leave the lobster out?' Anyway, your good friends remember what you can't or don't eat."

—Dorothy Kalins, writer and the founding editor of *Saveur* magazine

CHIPPING AWAY AT AN OLD FOOD MYTH

You know those rumors you've heard about Pringles potato chips containing sawdust and ground-up newspapers? The truth is even worse. It turns out that Pringles are so short on potatoes that they don't qualify as potato chips, according to an appellate court tax ruling in the United Kingdom (where chips are known as "crisps"). With 42 percent potato content, 33 percent flour and fat, and 25 percent "other," Pringles fall short of the necessary "potatoness" required to exempt them from the government's 15 percent value-added tax. Reporting the story, *Barron's Online* said, "A British court determined to answer one of the questions that has dogged human understanding since man emerged from the primordial ooze: What the heck is a Pringle, anyway?"

7

BE
PATIENT

[MEDICAL CENTER]

Who needs medical school? Thanks to a healthy dose of Dr. Sanjay Gupta, WebMD, and *Grey's Anatomy*, you can confidently offer second opinions first. ("It's not an allergy, Doctor. I know how an allergy would present.") After a two-minute Google search, you can ask your doctor what made him go to Grenada for medical school. Bragging rights include knowing your doctor's cell phone number and e-mail address. Then he or she can instantly turn around and tell the world what a nosy pain you are on a medical weblog where doctors vent about their patients.

Medical practices may be private, but everything else is very public. Why do we need to take pictures of our scars and put them on our iPhones to whip out and show everyone over lunch? (Nothing sours a Chinese chicken salad like close-ups of a C-section, two days post-op.) Is there no hospital that won't leak confidential celeb records to TMZ or Gawker?

"Public health" issues take on new meaning, thanks to our healthy appetite for anything that happens to someone else. Especially if it's bad.

While reality has led us to believe that medical professionals are a little flawed, reality TV and advertising have raised our expectations for what they can accomplish. With the right trainer and nutritionist and a TV camera on you at all times, you can lose half your body weight in just one prime-time season! A plastic surgeon with impressive surgical *and* Hollywood credentials will lift your eyes, lower your age, and lipo you into skinny jeans!

We're not the only ones benefiting from modern medicine. Our pets get PET scans. They take Prozac. They get peticures. They have acupuncture. They get braces to correct an overbite. Dogs have face-lifts, nose jobs, and tummy tucks to conform to the "breed standard." Cats have kidney transplants. We cater to our pets' psychological well-being with spas that offer "an open cage-free environment where your pet is free to socialize while waiting to be styled." And for $150,000, a South Korean company agreed to clone a California woman's pit bull, Booger.

Feel a migraine coming on?

You'll feel better fast after a quick consultation with a leading dermatologist, a social worker, a pharmacist, an outpatient-care coordinator to a prominent plastic surgeon, a cosmetic dentist, the vice president at EverydayHealth.com, the sports chiropractor for the New York Giants, a gynecologist who's the chairman of an in vitro fertilization program, and a registered nurse who doesn't suffer fools. ⇨

Is an anti-wrinkle injection (made of pig collagen) kosher?
"Yes, it has been approved by a rabbi. Kosher is dietary. So a porcine heart valve or an anti-wrinkle injection made of pig collagen is acceptable because you're not eating it. It doesn't interfere with kosher laws." —A DERMATOLOGIST with a leading teaching hospital who is herself Jewish

Your doctor offers you a discount on your Lasik operation or Botox procedure if you'll post a ten-minute video of the procedure on YouTube, along with your rave review and a link to the doctor's website. Do you jump at the deal?
"I'd continue bargaining until the operation is offered gratis, along with any necessary follow-up work." —A WOMAN who works with much younger people and who is tempted

You Google your doctor and learn that his ex-wife has issued a restraining order against him. Should you cancel the appointment it took you two months to get?
"Don't cancel the appointment. Just be guided by these three caveats:
1. The restraining order, a popular tool during nasty, vindictive divorces, may not have any basis in reality.
2. Make sure there's a nurse in the examination room with you.
3. Restrain yourself—and don't date him if he asks."
—MOLLY-JANE RUBINGER, a Massachusetts social worker

You hear about a new genetic test that can tell where your toddler's future athletic ability may lie. Should you wait to find out or should you start training your potential triathlete right now?

"Genetics can't tell you some of the key components for making a great athlete: attitude, energy, enthusiasm, drive. And it doesn't tell you what we know as doctors: Some bodies are injury-prone, so structural testing is as important as genetic testing. The inadequacies of the test aren't the only issue. Many parents already live vicariously through their children; this will contribute to more of that. You'll be saying, 'Hey, you're supposed to be a great runner. Why aren't you winning more races?' There's much more of a downside than an upside as far as I am concerned." —ROB DESTEFANO, DC, sports chiropractor for the New York Giants and author of *Muscle Medicine*

"At that age it's not about talent, it's about fun. No child should be deprived of Saturday mornings on the athletic field

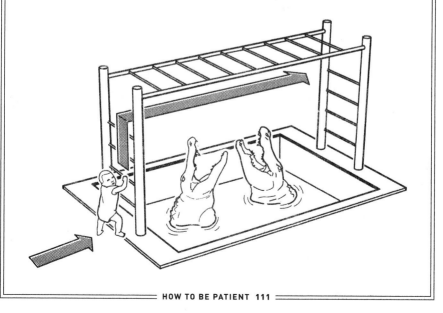

with the camaraderie of being on a team and the thrill of a cheering sideline (even if it's just Mom or Dad)."
—Kim Everett, a middle school lacrosse coach and former All-American lacrosse player

You take your dog to the vet to get his teeth cleaned. The receptionist says, "For another twenty-five dollars, we can give you the Total Comfort Care. The animal feels no pain." Is there any way to say no without looking completely heartless?
"In fact, dogs are better off at the dentist than people are, since they're out like a light for every procedure. Don't get scammed!" —Ellen Carlin, DVM

Now that CVS is everyone's local pharmacy, picking up your prescription can lead to a very public announcement of your chlamydia. Are pharmacists trained to shout? Is there any way to protect your privacy?
"It's not just a lack of respect, it's a violation of the law. National HIPAA laws protect patients' privacy. Because of these laws, we can't even tell a husband what medicine his wife is taking. So you have every right to say something. What should you say? If it were my regular pharmacist, I would just say, 'In the future, I would like you not to call out my meds in front of other people.'" —Bill McPadden, pharmacist at the Apthorp Pharmacy in New York City
To avoid the situation completely: "Switch to mail order, and report the guy (women are never that crass) to the state pharmacy board." —Donna Evans Hirsch, RN

SMOOTH AS A BABY'S, UM . . .

Put on a few pounds lately? Feeling sluggish or looking a bit older than you'd like? Pop into any Japanese pharmacy and for less than ten dollars, you can pick up a bottle of pig placenta. The rejuvenating powers of porcine afterbirth are legendary across Japan, although it hasn't earned the blessing of our Food and Drug Administration. Manufacturer Nihon Sofuken now offers placenta in pill, jelly, or beverage form, face mask or skin cream, and promises everything from a "nonsurgical face-lift" to a natural remedy for menopausal symptoms. A delicate peach flavoring is added to sweeten its appeal.

What does it mean if a plastic surgeon rejects you? Does he or she see you as impossibly ugly, particularly litigious, or an unrealistic perfectionist?

"It could be any of the above, so try to think it's the 'you're too young and beautiful' reason. But there could be some other red flag—like your health or the fact that what you are asking for is not a procedure this doctor feels best qualified to perform." —A LEADING DERMATOLOGIST at a major teaching hospital who regularly makes "Top Doctors" lists

"Don't be offended and don't expect an answer. This doctor might be on a chin-implant hiatus because he or she is doing a clinical trial in eye lifts." —A CONTRIBUTING EDITOR at *InStyle* magazine

You're sitting in an airplane next to a man who tells you he's a dermatologist. Is it okay to ask him to take just a quick look at that scaly thing on your neck?

"The first time someone asked me that kind of question, I was a young doctor serving in the air force. I was in the commissary when an officer saw me with my shopping cart and called out down the aisle, 'Hey, Doc—can you look at this rash?' and started pulling his pants down. Now, that was pretty embarrassing (I quickly told him it looked like something I needed to see in the office), but generally, I'm fine with someone asking me for my opinion. I went into medical school to help people. So I will take a look. If I were on a plane and I had something bothering me, I'd ask, 'What do you think it is?' or 'Should I see a dermatologist?' Legal liability is a potential issue, but to me looking at something on your seatmate's neck is the same as 'Do you stop on the side of the road to help someone in a car accident?'" —RON SHELTON, MD, dermatologic surgeon of the New York Aesthetic Consultants (TheNyac .com) and associate clinical professor, Department of Dermatology, Mount Sinai Medical Center

During your sonogram, the technician launches into a long story about how her son is a drug addict and her ex-husband is a drunk. She then adds that everyone in this practice thinks that *your* doctor is a real complainer who doesn't pull her own weight. Your response?
"Stop her with a brief exclamation of disbelief (e.g., 'Yeesh!'). Then redirect her by asking her to clarify whether you are looking at your baby's foot or kidney." —NATALIE BAUMGARTNER, principal at a business-psychology consulting firm that helps companies behave more professionally

You know your dog is special—quite possibly a distant relative of Marie Antoinette's papillon or Queen Elizabeth's regal Corgis. Don't you want to know? Should you spring for DNA testing (CanineHeritage.com) to find out what kind of dog your regal pet really is?

"Don't be seduced by any of this. If you love your dog, that's all you need to know. Take your $119.95, donate it to an animal shelter, and save a life." —JAKE KLEIN, an Oakland, California, animal shelter volunteer

A friend is looking quite a bit younger and, frankly, better. Should you/can you/must you ask if she's had work done?

"By all means ask, but be diplomatic. If you're comfortable, you could venture something like 'Wow, you look amazing. Special cream? Peel? Botox? Plastic surgery? Love? Great genes?' That way, your friend can tell you whatever she wants to." —A PSYCHOTHERAPIST who has counseled women both before and after elective surgery

"Some women are very open about it. Some are secretive. But if a woman does tell you that she has had work done, she'll also share with you who her doctor was."
—ALEXANDRA FRANCO, outpatient-care coordinator for a prominent Manhattan plastic surgeon who needs no publicist to get great publicity through magazine articles, medical awards, and word-of-mouth referrals

During college, you donated your eggs to an infertile couple for $10,000. Should you tell your parents or the person you may ultimately marry?

"No. Your body is your own. It has no impact on your parents. You are not obligated to disclose your donation to your spouse, either. If you are healthy, your donation will have no impact on your future fertility." —GYNECOLOGIST PETER CASSON, MD, who is board certified in reproductive endocrinology and the chairman of his clinic's in vitro fertilization program

"Saying nothing to anyone is entirely valid. It's between you and your conscience, and you don't owe this information to anyone." —A FERTILITY COUNSELOR in Austin, Texas

Your new dentist serves wine in his waiting room. When you ask why, he tells you it is to put his patients at ease. Is it okay to sip a glass of chardonnay, get numbed with novocaine, then drive home?

"Maybe in a salon or a spa, but absolutely not in a dental office. It's risky for the patient who may be taking other medications that aren't compatible with alcohol, as well as for the doctor, who may be crossing legal boundaries. A much better idea would be a cup of decaf cappuccino or chamomile tea. If you're really nervous, talk to your doctor about prescribing an anti-anxiety medication to take ahead of time or using nitrous oxide during the treatment." —MAL BRAVERMAN, MD, past president of the New York chapter of the American Academy of Cosmetic Dentistry

Your sore throat leads you to WebMD. A two-minute search convinces you that you have swine flu. How can you tell if it's real or if it's a real case of cyberchrondria?

"Take a deep breath, relax, and step away from the keyboard. The Web has a lot of health information and misinformation. Nothing replaces a call or visit to the doctor if you have a health concern." —TONY BRANCATO, vice president at Everyday Health.com

KINDA MAKES YOU
NOSTALGIC FOR DIPHTHERIA

Today you can suffer from a host of ailments for which there's no quick diagnostic test, no antibiotic to prevent complications, and no face mask or quarantine to halt the spread.

There's earbud-related hearing loss, resulting from turning up the volume to hear your music or phone, since earbuds don't cancel out background noise.

Watch out for e-thrombosis, a condition related to deep vein thrombosis; in e-thrombosis, blood clots form in the deep veins of people who spend long amounts of time in front of a computer without moving.

Can you spot the symptoms of orthorexia nervosa? A steady diet of scary news stories has raised our awareness of the risks of mercury-laden fish and pesticide-sprayed strawberries. But if you suffer from this eating disorder, your obsession with eating healthful foods makes you create a strict diet from which you won't deviate in your quest to achieve nutritional purity.

A rash of social anxiety disorder shows that even your friends can make you sick. Now that everyone is Facebooking, texting, and tweeting to his or her heart's content, this morbid fear of being watched and judged by others takes on technologically terrifying dimensions.

You are a vegetarian. Your dog isn't. To keep him as healthy as possible, is it up to you to make Sampson see the light?

From the enlightened nutrition expert: "Dogs descended from carnivorous wolves but evolved to be omnivores, which is one of the reasons we get along so well with them. Dogs like to eat meat, but they like eating everything else, too, and can get the nutrients they need from grains, beans, and other vegetables. Although the jury is still very much out on whether a meat-free diet is ideal, plenty of commercial vegetarian dog foods are on the market. Choose products labeled as complete and balanced for your dog's stage of life as demonstrated by feeding trials. Otherwise, if you want your dog to eat the same foods you do, just be sure to supplement with appropriate vitamins and minerals." —MARION NESTLE, Paulette Goddard Professor in the Department of Nutrition, Food Studies, and Public Health at New York University, author of *Pet Food Politics,* and coauthor of the forthcoming book *What Pets Eat*

From the passionate animal rights activist: "Whether or not I should impose my vegetarian diet on my pets has been a dilemma my animal-loving friends and I have long debated. My ever-evolving decision as to what to feed my dogs (and cats) is a complicated compromise and, when I discuss it with other animal welfare advocates, a controversial one. I am vegetarian primarily for humane reasons. I want my personal diet to inflict as little suffering on other animals as possible— animals including people. Yet I still feed my dogs meat. My choice for them balances my humane desires with what I believe is best for their health. While I would love for my dogs to be fully vegetarian, I haven't yet made the complete switch. I'm waiting to be convinced that this is the right thing to do."
—INGRID NEWKIRK, president and cofounder of People for the Ethical Treatment of Animals (PETA), the largest animal rights organization in the world

You've recently relocated and need a dentist. Two of the most prominent dentists in town are named "Dr. Fear" and "Dr. Payne." You don't believe that names are destiny, but is one of these the dentist for you?
"I thought it was a joke. These definitely wouldn't be the first names I would pick if I was going through the Yellow Pages. But if they came highly recommended, I would. Maybe."
—A NEWLY ARRIVED POSTDOC at the University of Michigan in Ann Arbor who encountered this situation

"I spotted a shingle for 'Dr. Plaque' when I moved to San Francisco and decided this was meant to be." —A WRITER who (almost) believes that a clever name can be as important as the right credentials

THE GIRL CAN'T HELP IT

A healthy twenty-six-year-old publicist from Miami with a huge crush on a sexy real estate agent she had just begun to date suddenly found herself in the hospital for observation. Her doctor was concerned because she was experiencing an irregular heartbeat, so he had her hooked up to a sophisticated and extremely sensitive heart monitor. In midafternoon, as she was dozing, there was a knock on the door and in walked her crush, carrying a big bouquet of roses. He smiled. She smiled back. Her heart skipped a beat—or two or three—then raced furiously and set off the heart monitor. He smiled. She blushed. Her doctor's diagnosis: a very mild arrhythmia and a severe case of love.

You're invited to a Botox party. Is this insulting or exciting? What should you bring the hostess?

"Not insulting in the slightest! People these days use Botox just as much for wrinkle prevention as wrinkle treatment. So no matter how furrowed your brow, consider the invitation a compliment. After all, the hostess probably assumes you've already jumped on the Botox bandwagon because you look so damn good. If you attend, show up with an antioxidant-themed token like gourmet dark chocolates and a pomegranate scrub." —POLLY BLITZER, editor in chief of BeautyBlitz.com

8

HOW TO

GET THROUGH THE
DAY
[FROM BOOK GROUPS
TO BARISTAS]

Every day, the everyday seems a little more puzzling. Manners are out the window. Ditto privacy. No topic is too far off-limits. Oh, and everyone's an expert and feels free to comment. Attorney Bob Bruno was walking his soft-coated dog, Sylvie—a rarely seen variation on an already exotic dog—when a passerby stopped him and asked, "Hey, what kind of dog is that?" "She's a Chinese crested," Bob responded politely. The stranger promptly corrected him: "No, she's not."

Your next-door neighbor, seeing your one-month-old son for the first time, says, "Oh, I thought he'd be cuter."

Are there any opinions we shouldn't share? Are there any questions too inappropriate or intrusive? "How did you feel when you found out that your sister was involved in the kinky sex scandal with the congressman?" asks a newscaster. "Have you thought of going on the Chubby Chasers dating site?" says a TV talk show host. "Then you wouldn't have to try to lose that weight!"

And is there some reason we now need our native language to be translated? From a fashion website: "In the solar system of fashion trends, if hemlines and silhouettes act like Jupiter and Saturn, denim is more like Mercury. . . . Happily you don't have to understand Kepler's laws of planetary motion to appreciate the current light-wash denim craze" (from WhoWhatWear.com).

Every day, just keeping up can get you down. There's the enviro-trend question: Do you need "sustainable swimwear"? And what exactly is it sustaining? There's the green-chic question: Do you want the classic Swedish massage or "the organic Amazonian babassu-oil crème massage?" There's the "how simply to simplify your life" question: Your significant other wants to give you a bike for your birthday. Do you dare ask for the Fendi city bike that's just under $6,000 and comes with a GPS holder and a fully outfitted picnic basket?

And now that boundaries are eroding by the minute, is it healthy candor or TMI to announce, "We're trying to have a baby but my husband's sperm count is low" at a cocktail party or for teenagers to wear T-shirts that say, "You're worth waiting for. So am I"?

Thank God for the military, the last bastion of "don't ask, don't tell." For those not in uniform, expert advice for life du jour comes from a human resources manager, a veterinarian, an eco-designer, a communications expert, a book-group facilitator, a certified conditioning specialist, and an intrepid road warrior. ⇨

Which is worse: falling asleep during a classical music concert or having your cell phone go off?

On one hand: "Having your cell phone go off during a concert is always worse. Unless you're a snorer (in which case, bring a date who can nudge you), sleeping rarely disrupts anyone except for you—and let's be honest, we've all been there. There is no excuse for not turning off your cell phone—it's the easiest thing in the world to do, and something that they have specifically asked you to do at the start of the concert. You may not be able to fight the biological urge to get some shut-eye around the fifth movement of Mahler's Third Symphony, but you can absolutely avoid adding accompaniment by Nokia." —AN ASSISTANT STAGE DIRECTOR whose grandfather was the cultural commissioner of New York City

On the other hand: "Snoozing is worse. It is just so personally embarrassing (the nodding head, the open mouth, the slack features). The phone is awful, and ultimately more disruptive, but you can always hope others will attribute it to a neighbor. Also, the phone ring is an isolated incident of rudeness, whereas the catnap is a sustained state of rudeness." —A WOMAN WHO HAS A SUBSCRIPTION to the opera, the ballet, and the local theater group

You're in Starbucks, where the language is "tall, grande, venti." Your barista asks what size skim latte you want and you say, "Small." Is this a small blow against the coy Starbucks vernacular or just an annoying answer to a busy barista?

It's not a problem. "It's a normal answer that the barista must hear all the time. It's like kids whose parents speak a language other than English who understand the parents' native

language but answer in English. It's fine for both: They speak the language that is most comfortable for them, and understand the language that the other uses. 'Tall, grande, and venti' is Starbucks for 'small, medium, and large.'"
—DEBORAH TANNEN, author of the *New York Times* bestseller *You Just Don't Understand*

It's a problem. "Use the Starbucks language if you know it. Doing otherwise only makes life that much harder for the poor hourly wage barista taking your order, and inconveniences the people waiting behind you. If you want to make a point to Starbucks, then tell their executives, write to their customer feedback site, scribble an editorial, put up a blog entry, figure out some other clever and effective response—or simply buy your coffee elsewhere, perhaps at a local independent. Gratuitous hassling of hourly employees—whether at Starbucks or your bank, and especially the poor souls working in call centers—is always very bad form. Don't let your annoyance with the Man translate into rude behavior to others who might be even more oppressed than you are. At the extreme, it is this sort of flawed thinking that causes rioters to run wild and, in their anger at some distant oppressor, to vandalize their neighbors' cars and damage the storefronts of the local shops they depend on. Even small acts of rebellion require careful aim, lest they simply make a situation worse."
—PAUL SAFFO, a technology forecaster and futurist who teaches at Stanford University

As you prepare to board, the screener at Heathrow inspects your passport and says, "Wow, you don't look that old!" Are you flattered or insulted? And what can you/should you say?

"I'd far prefer this scenario to the alternative: the Heathrow screener looking at my passport and saying, 'Geez, I could have sworn you were older.' I use situations like this one, which have happened more than once, to fish for more compliments: 'Oh really? How old do I look?' Even age-related comments that could be construed as rude don't normally bother me because I'm not hung up on age. Your attitude, far more than your age, is what defines you. The way to overcome fear of aging is to make the most of every minute, so that you don't wake up one day with regrets for what might have been. Comments about my wrinkles I can deal with. But someone suggesting I've lived a life of missed opportunities? Now, that would haunt me." —NANCY GRAHAM, editor of *AARP: The Magazine*

You're out for drinks with friends from work and everyone is comparing salaries. With everything out on the table, do you need to chime in?
"No. Just listen and gain what you can from their willingness to spill. This is great ammo that you may be able to use to your advantage in future salary negotiations. You don't have to be stuffy or prim about it. Humor helps: 'I get paid a tiny bit less than an hourly worker at McDonald's . . . but the coffee in our company cafeteria rocks!'" —VICKY OLIVER, a career expert and the author of *Bad Bosses, Crazy Coworkers and Other Office Idiots*

"Never a good idea. If you earn more, people wonder why you didn't get them nicer Christmas gifts. If you earn less, people wonder why you're going to Saint Croix on vacation. Better to be a mystery." —ALICE LIU, a researcher for a major cable station in San Diego

TO ADVERTISE HERE CALL: 1-800-675-0781

You've always wanted to go into advertising. And you will—in a visible and lucrative way—just by agreeing to shave your head and display an advertiser's message on a temporary tattoo. Is becoming a "cranial billboard" a creative way to pay the rent? A good career move?

"Not if the product is Rogaine. Seriously, it's fine. People have been selling their bodies as billboards since before Lacoste invented the alligator. So, why not? If you've got a nice-shaped head and look good bald . . . and you could use the money—go for it. But be sure to engage in only supportive discussions regarding the brand; you gotta have some ethics."
—CHRISTOPHER REINTZ, senior partner, Ogilvy & Mather

Do you need to tell a prospective employer that you sued your last employer? Do you need *not* to? Is honesty the best policy?
"You are under no legal or moral obligation to do so. But don't lie if you're asked the direct question. And don't be surprised if the company does a background check and finds out anyway." —DOTTI TEMPLETON, management consultant at a major national human resources consulting firm

"If the litigation will negatively affect your job performance or your prospective employer's business, then it should be revealed." —ATTORNEY LORI FINSTERWALD of Schillinger & Finsterwald

YOU CAN'T TAKE IT WITH YOU

Ironically, some people who've had cosmetic work done in life may undergo one last procedure after death. Free! "I require that the mortuary remove any kind of silicone implant before the body is delivered here for cremation," says Aida Bobadilla, manager of the Los Angeles Odd Fellows Cemetery and Crematorium. "Whether it's in the breast or the calf or the bicep or the cheek or wherever. After cremation, some silicone implants remain. It's like a glob of gelatin. There's no easy way to clean the floor of the cremation chamber."

You see an ad for Saks Fifth Avenue featuring "aggressive shoes" and "reformed polos." Are your current clothes sending the wrong message or is this just a retailer's way to boost business when people aren't buying?

"The ad actually raises more questions. Could an unrepentant embezzler or an incarcerated Ponzi schemer who still won't tell where he hid the money even *buy* a reformed polo? Could they wear it when they have a court date to improve their appearance? Should Saks even sell it to them? And wouldn't it be wrong for, say, the head of Greenpeace to buy an *aggressive* pair of shoes? Language, like clothes, is of the moment and fun to mix and match. You might be shy and retiring, for example, but that doesn't mean you can't be fashion-forward."
—A JOURNALIST who writes an advertising column for a trade paper

"Aggressive *running* shoes would be great. My life is a treadmill." —A CREATIVE DIRECTOR at a major advertising agency

You're all for going green and have zero-VOC paint for your home, a compost heap, solar panels, organic fruit and meat, a Prius. But how can you protect the planet and at the same time protect your dye-free pure-white organic sofa against muddy paws, projectile vomiting, and sulfite-free biodynamic red wine? (Is Scotchgard a solution or a sin?)

It's not easy being green. "Steer clear of pales, creams, whites, beiges. Go darker. If you have dirty children, buy patterned fabric for your sofa. For muddy paws, keep an organic towel at the front and back doors—it not only cleans off the dog, it also keeps outside toxins from coming in. Forget Scotchgard! Use organic cleaning products instead. And adopt the rules we have: No eating in the living room. And no red wine in the house." —LISA SHARKEY, author of *Dreaming Green: Eco-Fabulous Homes Designed to Inspire* and mother of one dog and three kids

"It's a lot easier than you think. There's no reason you can't be eco-gorgeous and eco-conscious. Get the sofa. Just make sure it has washable slipcovers. And of course you have to have red wine. Open that bottle of malbec and enjoy it!" —CAROL HELMS, design consultant

The voice of eco-advice on an environmental website ("Ask Umbra" at Grist.org) turns out not to be real. She is, instead, a fictional amalgam of the website's creators. Can you trust real advice from a virtual adviser?

"No advice should be trusted without some external affirmation of reliability, but the fact that an adviser is fictitious is by itself not a reason to dismiss the advice. We have a long history of wise fictional advisers worthy of our trust: Poor Richard (as in Ben Franklin's *Almanack*), Mr. Dooley (F. P.

Dunne's marvelous fictional wise everyman who appeared in the *Chicago Post* in the late 1800s and early 1900s), and Dear Abby (Abigail Van Buren was a fictional byline invented by Pauline Phillips and later shared with her daughter, Jeanne Phillips). Real advisers don't necessarily give reliable advice, and fictional advisers don't necessarily give poor advice. And fictional advisers backed by a team (like Dear Abby) may give better advice than the best of real advisers. You should always seek counsel widely, and then think—and verify—for yourself." —PAUL SAFFO, a technology forecaster and futurist who teaches at Stanford University

Today's ideal look for women includes Madonna's tight lats, Rene Russo's muscled legs, and Michelle Obama's taut biceps. Is sculpting the new walking? How do you know if it's time to trade in your Reeboks for a personal trainer?

"Women are no longer content to be just 'skinny' or 'slim'; they want muscle tone and definition. To achieve this sexy 'alpha female' body, focus on strength-training exercises designed to build lean, sculpted muscle, and stop fearing the weights. Shorten your cardio workouts dramatically by implementing short-burst, fat-melting interval cardio training. Eat plenty of lean, body-building protein and lots of fresh fruits and vegetables to get the energy and nutrition needed to function at your optimum level." —certified strength and conditioning specialist RYLAN DUGGAN, whose GoSleeveless.com website gives women targeted exercise and nutritional tools

MELANCOLLIE

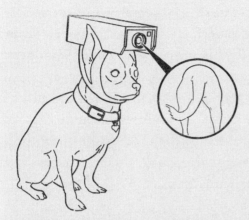

Your dog walker swears he gives your dog a workout worthy of Lance Armstrong. But how would you know? What if the dog walker is like the one—*or is the one!*— your friend saw sleeping on a bench while his furry charge just ambled aimlessly around the dog park? Now you can buy the Snif Tag (Sniftag.com), hailed by the *New York Times* as "the equivalent of the baby cam for neurotic dog owners." It attaches to your dog's collar and monitors what Rufus is up to—running, sleeping, catching a Frisbee, flirting with that cute springer spaniel—and records this so you can download it all later on your home computer.

Your friends have blogs for their pets and blog every day. If you really love Sparky, shouldn't you?

"Yes. Dogs are people too." —A WOMAN whose Christmas cards always feature her dogs in full Santa Claus regalia

"I would if I thought someone wanted to read the updates of my cats' daily adventures of sleep, switch chairs, sleep, eat, switch chairs." —PATRICIA DOHERTY, DVM and cat lover

You already tip the taxi driver, the doorman, the hairstylist, the coat-check lady, the curbside check-in baggage handler, the shoe-shine guy. Is there some reason why there is now a tip box at your dry cleaner, your deli, your florist? What is the rationale? Should you yield to the pressure? What's your tipping point?

"They do it because they can. But honestly, I don't feel guilty when I don't tip the florist. I am more than happy to tip well for service that goes above and beyond. But if someone is serving me an ice cream cone, how far 'above and beyond' can they go putting a scoop of ice cream into the cone?"

—THE FOUNDER OF BUSYMOM.NET, a popular blog that often deals with everyday issues and conundrums

Travel is the new food: à la carte and potentially very pricey. Should your choice of an airline depend on who's going to charge you extra for a direct flight, a choice seat, more legroom, checking your bag, a stale biscotti, changing your flight, or "letting you" use the bathroom?

"Fees are like mildew: Once they show up, they never go away. Ultimately, you have to decide what's important to you. If you're in a rush, it might be worth paying more for a nonstop flight. If you're six foot six, extra legroom is a steal at $10. (My general rule: The longer the flight, the more likely I am to care about a better in-flight experience.) The trick is to avoid putting yourself in a position where you're at the airline's mercy. Bring your own food and you'll never be so hungry that you have to overpay for the inedible. Use the facilities at the airport—especially if you're flying Ryanair—and you won't need to pay for the privilege of visiting the plane's lavatory. Pack light enough to carry on and you'll save yourself not only $25 (on most U.S. airlines) but also time at the baggage carousel." —ERIK TORKELLS, an editor for TripAdvisor .com, the founder of *Girlfriend Getaways* magazine, and the editor of three travel books

It's a $1,500 dress that will be worn only once to a black-tie event. Is it okay to keep the tag on it (inside) and return it afterward if it's in perfect condition?
"Of course not! First, it is like stealing—you are preventing the store from selling that dress for as long as you have it in your hot little hands. Second, there is always a chance that it won't be in 'perfect condition'—accidents happen—and then you are out $1,500 that you didn't plan on. Third, this is why there are stores springing up that rent dresses for parties!" —red-carpet favorites MARK BADGLEY and JAMES MISCHKA of Badgley Mischka, hailed by *Vogue* as one of the "Top 10 American designers"

"It is looked on as a totally disgraceful practice by retailers, who are often forced to take back a 'new' dress that reeks of perfume and perspiration—and that they cannot resell. And how embarrassed would you feel if you were out in this dress and someone saw the price tag still attached?" —MARY ANN RESTIVO, fashion designer and emeritus board member of the Council of Fashion Designers of America

What's more *now*: letting your friends think your Prada bag is the real thing or being able to boast that you got your totally convincing knockoff on the street for $50?

"Even though I own a few expensive handbags, the trendier ones seem like a waste of money when you're only going to have them for a couple of years. There's also something unbelievably satisfying when a fashionista with a real bag comes up to you and compliments you on yours, thinking it's real, too. My policy with fake bags has always been the same: With boys, you never kiss and tell; with bags, you never 'fake and tell.'" —FRANCESCA DELAURENTIS, a young film executive in Los Angeles

"Let people think what they want to. Who would ever look at my tote bag and see that in the tiniest mouse type it says 'Goyarda,' not 'Goyard'!" —LAURIE BECKELMAN, founder of Beckelman + Capalino, advisers to arts organizations, and a well-dressed presence at everything from the Venice Biennale to a museum gala in Buenos Aires

You love giving presents to your nieces and nephews. But are you really expected to give gifts for the last day of camp, the first day of school, losing a tooth, getting braces, being an understudy in the school play, and all the other major milestones?

"My two-year-old son just graduated to underpants. Shall I send out an announcement and prep the thank-you notes for the deluge of gifts from caring friends and relatives? Will you be attending a party? If you go to a 'graduation' party or the 'ceremony'—regardless of the achievement or lack thereof—a gift is necessary. Otherwise, I would not send a gift. Kids love the attention, so you can show your love with a funny card, a phone call, or an e-mail." —A CONNECTICUT MOTHER of two

You've house-swapped your city apartment for a vacation at a contemporary beach house with state-of-the-art everything. Should you call the owners at seven A.M. on Saturday to admit that (1) you can't figure out how to use the professional cappuccino maker, (2) you need the number of a plumber who will come over and show you how to turn on the six-jet supersonic shower, and (3) you still can't find the door or drawer that hides the custom-made Sub-Zero?

"Just keep trying until you push the right button, turn the correct dial, or stumble over the door or drawer where the Sub-Zero lurks. Don't pick up that phone!" —LISA HIGGINS, executive editor, *Metropolitan Home* magazine

A friend tells you her divorce is now final. Do you offer your congratulations or condolences or . . . ?

"By the time it's final, the time for looking back is over, so be a glass-half-full friend and focus on all the joys of freedom and independence. Then fix her up with your hottest single friend." —ARIANNA HUFFINGTON, cofounder and editor in chief of the *Huffington Post*

"Don't ever say something like 'Good riddance to that loser!' At one point in her life, she wanted to marry the guy."
—A MARRIAGE COUNSELOR in Spokane, Washington

CAN YOU HEAR ME NOW?

Do noisy neighbors keep you up till all hours? Get back at them with the Revenge CD! Treat them to any of twenty earsplitting sound effects that include a drill, a party of two hundred revelers, an "outstanding" orgasm, a drum played by a child, an inhuman scream, a domestic squabble, doors banging, an unhappy dog, a garbage truck, a newborn, and a rooster's cock-a-doodle-doo. A set of earplugs comes with the CD for your use only. (Worldwidefred.com.)

You're in coach flying to Hong Kong. The minute you reach cruising altitude, the guy in front of you puts his seat so far back it cuts off your already tiny space. So you put your seat back to compensate. Forcing the person behind you to do the same thing. Forcing the person behind her . . . et cetera, et cetera, et cetera. How do you—how does anyone—stop the madness?

"I am a strong believer in proper social behavior among civilized people. So I do not crank my own seat all the way back in response, since that encroaches on the precious space of an innocent person behind me. However, I am also a believer in punishing social criminals. So every time I get up, I make sure to firmly jostle the headrest of the lout in front, hopefully when the lout is asleep. Then I apologize, insincerely. If we all did this in situations where a lout intrudes on our space, the message would get across. On a broader scale, I blame the rapacious airlines for designing seating space that does not take into account basic human needs. They literally could not legally transport cattle in so little space."

—JOE SHARKEY, business travel columnist for the *New York Times* and author of six books

Everyone in your book group wants to have a glass of chardonnay and talk about the book. One member, however, wants to talk about how the book relates to her marriage, has affected her sex life, and has become a major topic at her weekly group psychotherapy session. How to make it end happily ever after?
"Without a shared purpose and some clear ground rules, it's easy for one person (I call this member 'the Ayatollah') to hijack the group. So you all need to decide together: 'Is it drinks first? Books first? Then we socialize?' Have a model to follow and stick to it. And if someone won't get with the program, a couple of members need to find ways to rein him or her in. Say something like 'Doesn't what you just said sound exactly like that situation in Elizabeth Strout's new book? Why don't we read about it instead?' Reading is what validates the personal experience. And that's why you're there in the first place." —ESTHER BUSHELL, book-group facilitator

The discreet card (it's recycled paper, of course) in your hotel bathroom urges you to reuse your towels to "save the environment." Is it okay to wait until you get home to be green?
"Yes. I dutifully recycle at home, but when I am on a business trip, I want a fresh towel every day. I think the hotel's request to be green—while it saves water—is largely a ploy to save money on laundry." —FREDERICK NEAL, a frequent business traveler for a health-care services company

"It depends on what type of trip you're on and how long you're staying. If you're on a business trip, I don't think it takes too much energy to be a little mindful and not leave every single king-size bath sheet and hand towel and washcloth strewn on the floor after every use. But if you're on a long-awaited, much-deserved vacation, I think it's okay to let go a little bit and enjoy a few more fresh fluffy towels than you would at home. If, in your regular day-to-day life, you are generally thoughtful about things like water use and how your actions affect the environment and natural resources, enjoying some luxurious towel usage when you're on vacation is not the end of the world." —A WOMAN who works with a San Francisco nonprofit group that deals with environmental issues

You're at a party where a grandmotherly woman introduces herself as a "radical feminist separatist lesbian," another guest tells you he is a "chief experience officer," and yet another declines the duck mousse pâté, explaining that she's an "aspiring vegan." Is it enough for you to say, "Hi, I'm Pam. I sell lamps"?

"It's a store. I'm the owner. Simple objects and useful design speak for themselves. Why can't people do the same?" —ALTA TINGLE, founder and owner of The Gardener in Berkeley, California, a hugely successful store that has gotten rave reviews in every leading shelter magazine

You're walking down the street when you see her coming out of a restaurant. You can't believe it's who you think it is and she's just a few feet away from you. You've got your cell phone out, but before you take the picture you wonder: Is it okay to shoot Sarah Jessica Parker?

"No. Absolutely not. Celebs are allowed their privacy. Leave them alone if you see them during their normal day. If it's a screening or some sort of PR event, then it's fine to take a picture. That's a public moment and they expect it then. Same answer if you are thinking of asking a celeb if you can be in a picture with them. Don't ask. Let them have a life."

—ROGER SHERMAN, a Peabody Award–winning and Oscar-nominated filmmaker and photographer

9

HOW TO

DEAL

[WHEN THINGS THAT NEVER HAPPEN HAPPEN TO YOU]

Some situations we find ourselves in are so unexpected, and so bizarre, that they don't just leave us clueless—they leave us breathless.

If it hasn't happened to you already, it's only a matter of time before you're confronted with the unconventional, the incomprehensible, the inexplicable, the insane.

With friends: You're visiting for the holidays and the man of the house (who's in prison for embezzlement) calls collect so he can say "Merry Christmas" to all the guests individually.

At work: A job applicant you're considering offers to draw up a legal document making his employer his sole heir when he dies. "If I outlive you, my assets can be left to your family," he notes in the résumé he's posted on Craigslist.

With children: Your teenage daughter is excited to tell you that she knows what she wants for her birthday: "Eye jewels!" She hands you a magazine article about the funky new fashion accessories that hang from your contact lenses. "Don't worry," she assures you, "they won't affect my vision."

When there's good news: A birth announcement informs you that the baby is named Philomena3Jane, in a tribute to the cyberpunk classic *Neuromancer.*

When there's bad news: A colleague is sitting at her desk in front of her computer, weeping. Assuming that she has just received terrible news, you gently ask if there is anything you can do to help. She turns the computer screen to show you a picture of an ordinary-looking beagle. Crying inconsolably, she says, "It's Buffy. My beagle. He's still alive on VirtualPet Cemetery.org. Do you want to say hi to him or throw him a virtual Frisbee?" Do you hand her a virtual Kleenex?

When you're dating: His online dating profile seduces you

with his passion for "serving breakfast in bed—my amazing homemade organic pancakes—for the woman I love." On your second date, you are horrified to spot a spray can of something called Batter Blaster in his refrigerator. "Its unique, pressurized, patent-pending process lets you just point, blast and cook!" promises the website, BatterBlaster.com. Isn't it romantic?

And just about anywhere else: Alaska, which has the highest per capita number of rape cases in the United States, held a lottery to raise money for a group that helps victims of sexual abuse. The winning ticket for the $500,000 jackpot was . . . a twice-convicted sex offender. "It's not how we envisioned the story going," said Nancy Haag, executive director of the nonprofit organization Standing Together Against Rape based in Anchorage.

Sometimes the situation is so unprecedented that there is really only one place to turn. Being clued in is a whole lot easier when you're on the same page with experts like the inventor of testicular implants for dogs, a woman who saw her neighbor carted off in handcuffs, a celebrity TV star and author of *Class with the Countess,* the creator of a game that teaches safe cell phone use, a Peace Corps alumna, a head bartender, a reverend, and the irreverent. ⇨

After three Cosmos, the head of HR tells you which married colleague is dating your boss. What do you say/do/not do, and to whom?

"Stay above the fray. Anything said after three drinks should be filed away in that 'never to be disclosed' file and you should forget it was ever said. Mentioning the indiscretion to anyone—including the head of HR, the next day—could be dangerous. If he or she likes to dish, that barbed tongue may be aimed at you next." —VICKY OLIVER, a career expert and the author of *Bad Bosses, Crazy Coworkers and Other Office Idiots*

Your neighbor is carted away in handcuffs and the press is camped out in front of his house. Do you call his wife? Bring her a coffee cake? Go right on TMZ?

"I called his wife and asked if there was anything I could do for her, like shop (so she wouldn't have to face the press), hold her hand, ask her over (she could sneak out the back door), or whatever she needed, after my neighbor, a prominent criminal defense lawyer, was indicted for bribery." —A WOMAN who actually experienced something similar

You're at a celebratory dinner at a noisy, chic restaurant with a bunch of friends. In the middle of dinner, the guy next to you says in a low voice, "I've just come out." What do you say?

"I'd say, 'Are you happier? Do you feel comfortable telling the people at this table? Is there anyone I can help set you up with?'" —A SOPHISTICATED MAN with a nephew who dates transsexuals and whose mother married her French teacher so he could get a green card

You're at an upscale New York salon when in walks the wife of a disgraced celebrity whose mug shot you saw on last night's news. Should you smile sympathetically? Look away? Pretend you don't know?

"You don't want to embarrass her by mentioning a situation she might not choose to talk about. It's up to her to introduce the subject, not you. For these occasions, hairstylists that make house calls are the best option."

—COUNTESS LUANN DE LESSEPS, star of the Bravo TV series *The Real Housewives of New York City* and author of *Class with the Countess*

The reverend's cell phone rings as he is delivering the eulogy at your uncle's funeral. What should he, or the rest of you, do?

"Of course it is an embarrassment. But it isn't such a terrible thing for your congregation to know that you're human, too. So I would apologize and not make too big a deal of it. If I knew the family well, I might say something like 'Well, it wasn't God.' I think God has a sense of humor. Things of faith are to be taken seriously, but we can often handle them lightly." —REVEREND CHARLES SVENDSEN, interim pastor of Wilshire Presbyterian Church in Los Angeles

A woman is sitting in the back of a cab when the very attentive foreign-born driver turns around and says something that sounds like "You have really big tits!" Or maybe he said, "You have really big teeth." Does he lack boundaries or language skills? What does she say? And how much should she tip?

"I would probably take it as an opportunity for cultural exchange: Are teeth not that big where you come from?

Where are you from? Is malnutrition common there? Do you have the tooth fairy where you're from? Show an interest in his country and steer the conversation with innocent questions to defuse any possible tension that might have existed if indeed he had said 'tits.'" —A PEACE CORPS ALUMNA and law student who's been groped on three continents and in five languages

You're a fifty-something woman shopping at Club Monaco for a terrific pair of skinny pants for a party this weekend. As you browse the aisles, a cheerful salesperson comes up to you and says, "We have a section for the older, heavier woman." What should you say?

"'Are you on commission?' worked for me."
—ABIGAIL CHILLAK, a jewelry designer in Toronto and the shopper in question (who thinks of herself as younger and thinner)

Your neighbor has been putting off having his rottweiler neutered. One day he announces with pride that Brutus has been fixed—and now sports silicone testicular implants called Neuticles that are so convincing the dog still looks and feels like a "man." Should you be impressed?

"Yes. Canines are treasured members of the family. Neuticles are a perfectly safe and inexpensive option that allows a pet to retain identity and self-esteem." —GREGG A. MILLER, inventor of Neuticles, which are now used in thirty-two countries worldwide

"No. Anyone who is that obsessed with his dog's private parts must be covering up his own inadequacies." —A FEMALE VETERINARIAN whose male dog was neutered the conventional way

In keeping with your friends' minimalist taste, the guest-bathroom shower in their ultracontemporary new home has a huge window and no window treatment. So while you shower, you can look out and see all of the Great Smoky Mountains, and anyone on the front lawn can look in and see all of you. You take the world's fastest shower, a sudsy nightmare where you are crouched down in the dark, unable to tell the shampoo from the conditioner and too scared to turn on a light. Afterward, your gracious host asks, "So, did you enjoy your shower?" What can you possibly say to her?

"I put on quite a show. But I'm afraid I scared off every stray deer, raccoon, and new neighbor in the vicinity, as I'm sure I flashed them getting in and out of the shower. I guess you didn't know about privacy glass, where you can see out but they can't see in. It's in all the trendiest restaurant bathrooms—you might want to look into it."

—AN INTERIOR DESIGNER in Memphis, Tennessee

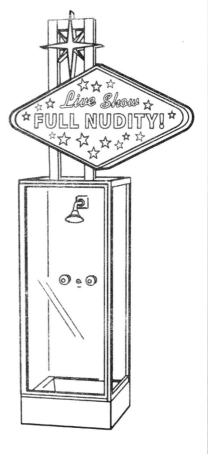

The guy on the bar stool next to you places an urn with his dog's ashes right next to your gin and tonic, which certainly does not lift your spirits. What can you—or the bartender—say, or do?

"My job is taking care of people, so I need to be aware of any situation at the bar. In this case, if I saw one guy who looked annoyed by the urn next to his drink and discovered that the guy with the ashes had just lost his beloved dog, I'd buy both a drink and we could toast the dog. I'd pour one for myself, too—I'm a dog lover." —JACK VESPA, head bartender at South Gate Bar in the Jumeirah Essex House

A business client, someone you barely know, is proud of her new breast implants. She lifts her shirt and says, "Touch them. Don't they feel real?" Can you? Should you? *Must* you?

"I'd smile and nod and say, 'You know, my expertise is only as a social worker [or investment adviser/decorator/beautician/ fill in the blank], so I'll just take your word for it. I'm glad you're so pleased, and I hope you enjoy them in good health.'" —A BOSTON SOCIAL WORKER

Two couples you know tell you that they lost all their savings to Bernie Madoff's Ponzi scheme. Do you introduce them? Throw a dinner party for them? Serve po'boys and chips? Bake financiers? Serve caviar and champagne, to make them feel better? Act like you lost money, too, even though you didn't?

"I would say nothing about the mutual misfortunes the two couples had faced but instead would connect other dots in their lives that would create common ground. I'd loosen

things up by pouring an easy-to-drink, not-too-special white wine. After an hour, with my guiding, I guarantee the couples will have found shared people, places, and interests, creating enough confidence and comfort for my next move: When the two couples begin to behave like old friends, I'll ask if people would prefer to drink a bottle of merlot or a pinot noir. Odds are ninety-nine to one that at least three of the four guests will choose pinot and I'll promise them something special. At that moment, I'll dig into my cellar and bring out a bottle of Ponzi Pinot Noir Reserve from Oregon's Willamette Valley."
—RESTAURATEUR DANNY MEYER, CEO of the Union Square Hospitality Group

"The less said, the better, unless the Madoff victims want to discuss their problems. So I would not introduce the two couples, at a dinner party or otherwise, because that would be tantamount to saying that their victimhood is, for me, their most important characteristic. Nor would I make light of the situation by serving po'boys or financiers. Finally, I would not act like I had lost money, too, because that's patronizing. I would try to empathize and express my regrets. If they were really good friends, I would ask if there was something I could do to help." —lawyer and food lover BOB LEVINE of New York and Paris, who blogs on BobbyJayOnFood.com

Which anniversary date should be celebrated by same-sex partners who have lived in a state where gay marriage is legal, several states that forbid it, and a state that legalized it and then allowed a popular referendum to deny it again?
"We celebrate our anniversary each year on July 8, the day my partner and I first met. We never envisioned recognized

domestic partnerships with benefits, civil unions, or that same-sex marriages would be legalized. Our date of meeting can never be taken away from us." —JOSEPH, who shares his heart and home with his partner of fifteen years

You get a call from your daughter's middle school guidance counselor letting you know that your eleven-year-old has been caught "sexting." Her cell phone, which was confiscated in class, has nude photos of herself that she was sending to boys on the soccer team. What do you say and do?

"As a parent, I think it's important to talk to your daughter about her self-esteem and try to understand what would cause her to make a decision like this. You will also need to address the issue of legality. Currently, both the sender and the receiver of nude photos of children under eighteen can fall under laws that apply to child pornography. The school will most likely have a policy on how to deal with the situation, which might include discipline for your daughter and those who received and passed on the photos. Until the laws catch up with technology in this area, the consequences can be very severe for what could be adolescent curiosity or naïveté. Your child will need your unconditional love and strong support." —JUDI WESTBERG-WARREN, president of Web Wise Kids (Web WiseKids.org), whose game It's Your Call is used by schools to teach teens about safe cell phone use

You're standing in the dog park, deep in thought, when someone's Dalmatian stops at your side and pees on your leg. What do you do?

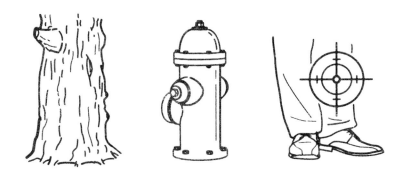

"It's *never* appropriate for you to discipline someone else's dog unless the dog is attacking you (or someone near you) and you need to intervene to save life or limb. Your best response is to make a mental note not to let yourself get lost in deep thought when you're in the dog park. After all, the dog park *is* a place where dogs are free to run around and pee on things."

—PAT MILLER, certified dog behavior consultant and pet trainer and author of four books, including *The Power of Positive Dog Training*

ACKNOWLEDGMENTS

To Doris Cooper, Rosy Ngo, Jane Treuhaft, Bonnie Thompson, Ashley Phillips, and Angelin Borsics. Never clueless; always savvy, smart, and supportive.

To Matthew Elblonk, our clued-in agent. Never baffled or bewildered.

CONTRIBUTORS

Among the experts who tell you *what to do when no one has a clue:*

JAMES ABEL, owner of an international event-planning and design firm; he has done weddings in locations from the British Virgin Islands to Maui to Manhattan.

ANTHONY DAVID ADAMS, cofounder of the education blog DetentionSlip .org, which was named one of the Top 25 blogs by *Time* magazine.

MARK BADGLEY AND JAMES MISCHKA, red-carpet favorites who, under the design label Badgley Mischka, have been hailed by *Vogue* as one of the "Top 10 American designers" for their glamorous, elegant evening wear and accessories.

CELIA BARBOUR, contributing editor at *O* magazine and a former writer for the *New York Times'* "Dining In" column.

RICK BAYLESS, chef and owner of Frontera Grill and Topolobampo, host of PBS's *Mexico: One Plate at a Time,* and winner of Bravo TV's *Top Chef Masters* competition.

POLLY BLITZER, editor in chief of BeautyBlitz.com and a consultant to *InStyle* magazine.

MARCY BLUM, wedding and event producer whose celebrity clients include everyone from Rockefellers to rock and roll's Billy and Katie Joel. Her bridal advice is often found in *InStyle Weddings, Modern Bride, Town & Country,* and the *New York Times*.

MICHAEL BOTTIGLIERO, wine expert at Chicago's Eno Wine Room.

TONY BRANCATO, vice president at EverydayHealth.com, a leader in online consumer health information.

MAL BRAVERMAN, MD, past president of the New York chapter of the American Academy of Cosmetic Dentistry, has been recognized in *New York* magazine's "Best Beauty Doctors" issue.

CHERIE BURBACH, the "Dating" feature writer for Suite101.com and the author of *Internet Dating Is Not Like Ordering a Pizza.*

ESTHER BUSHELL, a book-group facilitator whose opinions and perspectives are sought by leading publishers and who has made appearances on *Good Morning America* and National Public Radio. (LiteraryMatters.net)

ADA CALHOUN, editor in chief of Babble.com and author of *Instinctive Parenting.*

JOHN CARMON, owner of Carmon Community Funeral Homes in Windsor, Connecticut, and an early adopter of funeral webcasting technology.

KATE CARNEY, bridal sales consultant for the Jenny Yoo Collection, New York.

PETER CASSON, MD, a gynecologist who is board certified in reproductive endocrinology and is the chairman of his clinic's in vitro fertilization program.

ROBERT CLAGETT, dean of admissions at Middlebury College.

COLIN COWIE, event producer, designer, lifestyle authority, and author of seven bestselling books; his client list includes Oprah Winfrey, Nicole Kidman, and Sheikh Tamim Bin Hamad Al Thani, among others.

COUNTESS LUANN DE LESSEPS, star of Bravo TV's *The Real Housewives of New York City* and author of *Class with the Countess.*

CAROLINE DEL COL, a journalist and the executive editor of a national lifestyle magazine.

ROB DESTEFANO, DC, sports chiropractor for the New York Giants and author of *Muscle Medicine.*

RYLAN DUGGAN, certified strength and conditioning specialist who calls himself "the natural plastic surgeon." (GoSleeveless.com)

DIANE EHRENSAFT, PhD, a developmental and clinical psychologist in the San Francisco Bay Area and the author of *Mommies, Daddies, Donors, Surrogates.*

BEN FINKEL, founder and CEO of the online-community site Fluther.com.

HELEN FISHER, PhD, the relationship expert called "the dating guru" by *People* magazine, research professor at the Center for Human Evolution Studies at Rutgers University, and chief scientific adviser to Chemistry.com.

BETHENNY FRANKEL, natural-food chef, bestselling author of *Naturally Thin: Unleash Your Skinnygirl and Free Yourself from a Lifetime of Dieting*, and star of Bravo TV's *The Real Housewives of New York City*.

MEG FROST, Apple executive and founder of the award-winning website CuteOverload.com, called "the fuzziest, nicest blog on the planet" by CBS News.

FRANKLIN GETCHELL, co-owner and president of Moss, "arguably the best design store in America," according to the *New York Times*, and a mecca for sophisticated wedding shoppers in search of one-of-a-kind gifts.

NANCY GRAHAM, editor of *AARP: The Magazine*.

G. DORSEY GREEN, PhD, a psychologist in independent practice in Seattle, an adjunct clinical faculty member at The University of Washington, and a coauthor, with D. Merilee Clunis, PhD, of *The Lesbian Parenting Book*.

PILAR GUZMÁN, former editor in chief of *Cookie* magazine.

RON HAST, a funeral director and the publisher of *Mortuary Management* magazine.

LISA HIGGINS, executive editor of *Metropolitan Home* magazine.

ARIANNA HUFFINGTON, cofounder and editor in chief of the *Huffington Post*.

MARK HURST, founder of Creative Good and author of *Bit Literacy: Productivity in the Age of Information and E-mail Overload*.

DANIEL JONES, editor of the "Modern Love" column in the *New York Times*.

DOROTHY KALINS, writer and the founding editor of *Saveur* magazine.

EVAN MARC KATZ, author of *Why You're Still Single* and creator of the online dating system FindingTheOneOnline.com.

BEE KIM, founder of the popular wedding site Weddingbee.com.

ASHLEY KING, founder of BabymoonFinder.com.

CYNTHIA KRAUSE, MD, assistant clinical professor of gynecology, Mount Sinai Hospital, New York.

CORBY KUMMER, winner of five James Beard Awards and creator of *The Atlantic Monthly*'s food channel, Food.TheAtlantic.com

STEVE LEIFMAN, associate administrative judge in Miami-Dade County, Florida.

LOUIS LICARI, owner of hair salons in New York and Beverly Hills, beauty contributor to the *Today* show, and the star of NBC's *Ambush Makeover*.

ANITA LO, chef and co-owner of the New York restaurant Annisa and a finalist on Bravo TV's *Top Chef Masters*.

ALLAN MAYEFSKY, a partner in the law firm of Sheresky Aronson Mayefsky & Sloan and the president of the New York State chapter of the American Academy of Matrimonial Lawyers.

LISA MCCURDY, a San Francisco attorney who is an associate at the firm of Schiff Hardin, which represents the Animal Legal Defense Fund.

BILL MCPADDEN, pharmacist at the Apthorp Pharmacy in New York City, which has been in business since 1910.

DANNY MEYER, restaurateur and CEO of the Union Square Hospitality Group.

GREGG A. MILLER, inventor of Neuticles and the author of *Going . . . Going . . . Nuts!*

PAT MILLER, certified dog behavior consultant and pet trainer; author of four books, including *The Power of Positive Dog Training;* training editor for the *Whole Dog Journal;* and owner of Peaceable Paws in Hagerstown, Maryland.

JULIE MORGENSTERN, internationally renowned organizing and time-management expert and bestselling author of *Organizing from the Inside Out*, dubbed the "queen of putting people's lives in order" by *USA Today*.

SARA MOULTON, star of the PBS chef series *Sara's Weeknight Meals* and author of *Sara's Secrets for Weeknight Meals*.

MARION NESTLE, Paulette Goddard Professor in the Department of Nutrition, Food Studies, and Public Health at New York University, author of *Pet Food Politics,* and coauthor of the forthcoming book *What Pets Eat*.

INGRID NEWKIRK, president and cofounder of People for the Ethical Treatment of Animals (PETA).

VICKY OLIVER, a career expert and the author of *Bad Bosses, Crazy Coworkers and Other Office Idiots*.

RICH POLIAK, owner of Elements Restaurant & Enoteca in Napa, California.

CHRISTOPHER REINTZ, senior partner, Ogilvy & Mather.

MARY ANN RESTIVO, fashion designer and emeritus board member of the Council of Fashion Designers of America.

ARTHUR ROBIN, PhD, licensed psychologist, coauthor of *Your Defiant Teen,* and chief of psychology at Children's Hospital of Michigan in Detroit.

CARLEY RONEY, cofounder of America's leading wedding site, TheKnot.com, and author of *The Knot Book of Wedding Lists.*

PAUL SAFFO, a technology forecaster and futurist who teaches at Stanford University (Saffo.com).

PAMELA REDMOND SATRAN, coauthor of *Beyond Ava and Aiden, The Baby Name Bible,* and *Cool Names for Babies,* and cofounder of the online baby-name database Nameberry .com.

PEPPER SCHWARTZ, PhD, a University of Washington sociologist, the author of fourteen books about relationships, and a sexuality adviser for WebMD.

JOE SHARKEY, columnist for the *New York Times;* author of six books, including *High Anxiety;* and one of only seven people on a business jet who survived a midair collision with a 737 that killed all 154 passengers on the 737.

LISA SHARKEY, author of *Dreaming Green: Eco-Fabulous Homes Designed to Inspire.*

RON SHELTON, MD, dermatologic surgeon of the New York Aesthetic Consultants (TheNyac.com) and associate clinical professor, Department of Dermatology, Mount Sinai Medical Center.

ROGER SHERMAN, Peabody Award–winning and Oscar-nominated filmmaker and photographer and a founding member, with Ken Burns, of Florentine Films.

KIM SIBLEY, owner of Little Urbanites in Portland, Oregon, and LittleUrbanites.com.

JOYCE SLATON, editor of UrbanBaby San Francisco.

NANCY SLOTNICK, a love-life-management specialist who has consulted for JDate and whose website, Cablight.com, claims to help a woman find the man of her dreams in less than six months.

PATTI STANGER, star of the Bravo TV series *The Millionaire Matchmaker* and author of *Become Your Own Matchmaker.*

NANCY STEPHENS, an educator and activist who is on the executive board of directors of the Union of Concerned Scientists.

ROBERT W. SURLES, author of *Chef Bobo's Good Food Cookbook* and former instructor at the French Culinary Institute.

REVEREND CHARLES SVENDSEN, interim pastor of Wilshire Presbyterian Church in Los Angeles.

DAVID TANIS, head chef at Chez Panisse in Berkeley, California, and author of *A Platter of Figs.*

DEBORAH TANNEN, distinguished professor of linguistics at Georgetown University and author of *You Just Don't Understand* and *You Were Always Mom's Favorite.*

ALTA TINGLE, founder and owner of the Gardener, a chic home-goods shop in Berkeley, California.

ERIK TORKELLS, an editor for TripAdvisor.com, the founder of *Girlfriend Getaways* magazine, and the editor of three travel books.

JACK VESPA, head bartender at South Gate Bar in the Jumeirah Essex House.

JIN WANG, a San Francisco fashion designer whose contemporary collection includes bridal gowns and bridesmaids' dresses.

DONNA WARNER, editor in chief of *Metropolitan Home* magazine.

ARI WEINZWEIG, cofounding partner of the Zingerman's Community of Businesses in Ann Arbor, Michigan.

JUDI WESTBERG-WARREN, president of the national nonprofit organization Web Wise Kids (WebWiseKids.org).

MICHAEL WINERIP, a Pulitzer Prize–winning reporter for the *New York Times*, creator of the column "Generation B" for the *New York Times*, and author of *9 Highland Road.*

INDEX

moving in together, 50–51
by one's parents, 48
online dating sites, 49, 51, 54
paying for dates, 58
Skyping with date, 55
trust and privacy issues, 51
vegetarians, 104
while living with parents, 57
dentists, 116, 119
dermatologists, 113–14
divorce
changing name after, 67–68
deciding who gets the pet, 71
divorce lawyers, 69
divorce parties, 38
removing ex from family photos,
70
responding to news of, 135
doctors
asking free advice from, 113–14
Googling information on, 110
negotiating price with, 110
plastic surgeons, 113, 115
WebMD, 116–17
when to visit, 116–17
dogs
dead, ashes of, 71, 148
of divorced couple, 71
DNA testing and, 115
dog walkers for, 131
peeing on people's legs, 150–51
teeth cleaning for, 112
testicular implants for, 146
vegetarian diets for, 118–19

eco-friendly living, 129–30, 137–38
eggs, donating, 115–16

Facebook
being friended by ex, 68
friending new acquaintances,
52–53
incriminating photos on, 19–20,
42
food, 62. See also restaurants
foreigners, talking with, 145–46
funerals, 40–41, 70, 145

gays
children of, 65
coming out, 144
dating and, 53, 57–58
gay marriages, 69–70, 149–50
genetic testing, 111–12
gifts
Bar Mitzvah, 40
registering for, 42
wedding, 30, 31, 34, 38
when to send, 134
graduations, 68–69

hair appointments, 24
handbags, 133–34
hotel reservations, 22
house-swaps, 135

invitations, 32, 39
iPhones, 14, 20–22

jewelry, 67

kosher laws, 110

lawyers, divorce, 69
lesbians
children of, 78, 79
dating and, 53
lesbian marriages, 33, 53, 149–50

makeovers, 37, 71–72
marriage
gay, 69–70, 149–50
lesbian, 33, 53, 149–50
name changes after, 42–43, 67–68

nannycams, 88
neighbors, 23, 136, 144

parents
being honest with children, 64
at college graduations, 68–69
control over teenagers, 65, 66,
88–89
dating activities of, 48
prebaby getaways for, 78